Introduction

The Lemonade Stand series always takes on a life of its own. This holds true for Book 3. I wait to create the cover, the subtitle, and the back cover as the chapters begin to form, and the author community starts to engage and take ownership of the work. As I was wrapping up the chapters, I saw some interesting overlaps. I don't think this happens by accident.

Two authors reference Alice in Wonderland, a fictional tale that reflects much of today's reality. The orderly world vs. madness and the many varied characters encountered. Like Alice, we face many challenges in today's world, both real and perceived. Another chapter includes an analogy of the characters in The Wizard of Oz. Fairytales written long ago that still reflect adult realities.

You'll notice four authors are in real estate investment. Each of these authors had unique lemon obstacles to face. Real estate investing proved to be a lucrative option for these intelligent, hardworking, and passionate single women to be successful.

We have poignant stories of loss, family changes, unconditional love, and endurance. The book begins and ends with opposing sides of organ donation: a bittersweet topic of giving and receiving and all the joy and pain surrounding it—a second chance to live because someone else had to die.

The book has 11 chapters which was intentional. There are powerful lessons associated with (angel) number 11. The vibrational frequency of the number 11 is about symmetry and serenity. Its appearance is a reminder to maintain balance and trust your intuition. To know you are destined for greatness. It symbolizes the discovery of your authentic calling, taking responsibility for your life, and letting go of fear. It is a state of spiritual enlightenment where your heart and mind prepare for what's to come. Chapter 11 tells the story behind Michael Sigler's brief life on earth. A genuine angel among us.

The Lemonade Stand books create an unbreakable bond of authors sharing in a safe place and helping each other to grow in strength and confidence. I sincerely hope you enjoy reading these beautiful stories and take a lesson from each one. If you are interested in sharing your story, I welcome you to contact me.

Michelle Faust

hello@lemonadelegend.com

Table of Contents

Foreword

A disco ball is hundreds of pieces of broken glass put together to make a magical ball of light. Behind those pieces of glass is an impressionable and soft piece of styrofoam that is easily transformed with all those pieces when placed orderly on top. The styrofoam ball proudly displays its brilliance and reflects an awe-inspiring dance of light, bringing the attention of many to it. We are all styrofoam balls picking up our pieces and placing them on us the best we can or know.

We absorb bits and pieces of resilience through others, making us whole every day. Some of us understand, and some never do but believe me, we are all receiving and being molded perfectly by that magic. We may find that magic resilience in conversations, hanging out with others, watching/hearing of the seemingly seamless journey of others, or reading another's shared story.

No one's journey is seamless. No one. Like a sweater with words of wisdom or a witty crack causing a smile or laughter sewn on the front, but you turn it inside out, and it's a hot mess of hanging threads, tangled threads, and knots. Or perhaps some glue to keep things in place. There's maybe even some fabric to cover up the mess and avoid causing itchiness. If it's covered in sequins and doesn't have a liner, it's for sure itchy. One side of the sweater displays something that tells others more about us or displays a dance of lights within the sequins, while the underside is what lies beneath to create that beautiful display.

We, too, are sewn together. We are sewn together with beautifully intricate energy and light. Our experiences in life have made us unique in perfectly imperfect ways. Sometimes our energy drops, our light dims, or, hardest yet, both simultaneously. But we hear, see, and learn of others making it out of their darkest hours, and because we are all connected, we instinctively know we can too.

Michelle Faust understands all that wonderfulness, and she's on a passionate mission to:

1. Help others love an imperfect past that makes them so wonderful.

2. Cheerlead them to know how wonderful they truly are.

3. Share their light with others.

She helps others place those beautiful pieces of glass on in an orderly fashion and look at them with self-pride for what they endured.

I met Michelle a few years ago because a friend of mine, Sam Gibson (formerly Root), referred me to her. Sam is an author in the first The Lemonade Stand publication. Sam knew I had a story to share. I spoke with Michelle to great lengths, and she told me my story was impactful and needed to be out there to help others. But she didn't think we could get my story into one chapter. She then asked if I'd ever thought of writing my own book. Here I am over two years later, with her cheering and support as my publisher, and I'm a writer and author of a bestselling book.

She inspired me to get out there and share my light in ways I never thought of. She guided me to podcasts shows, YouTube channels, streaming TV, and more. Now I'm even doing speaking competitions and engagements. It's been an amazing whirlwind ride that I never foresaw. But that's just it; she helped me love ME even more. She encouraged ME to comfortably and gracefully love all of ME. She helped me understand that I had nothing to hide and that I MUST share my story to help others. The super-imperfect ME is a gem. I am literally a diamond in the rough. She came in and started chiseling away until I could see my brilliant light.

TLS3 is filled with powerful, must/read stories. Stories that will inspire and change lives. Shoot, I'm still thinking about having a chapter in a future Lemonade Stand to share my own business story. She's changing lives and bringing people together too! And I'm all about that. I've met so many incredible humans through Michelle.

Without polling the authors in TLS3, I can tell you without a doubt she's helped each and every one of these authors believe in themselves. She's helped them to learn to live an impactful life and to help others. She naturally inspired them to be more!

We are all connected; therefore, we thrive partly because of others. Brace yourself as you read the vulnerable stories of the people sharing their light in the following chapters.

Once again, a disco ball is hundreds of pieces of broken glass put together to make a magical ball of light. YOU'RE NOT BROKEN; YOU ARE A DISCO BALL.

Enjoy this Lemonade Stand of Disco Balls!

Live a Joyous Life! Share Your Light! Lots of Love and LUV!

Jenny DeBolt

Bestselling Author, Speaker, and Beacon of Joy

Suicide & Sequins; A Journey to a Joyous Life

A Second Chance

By John Weiman

I was drinking too much and couldn't stop. I didn't want to. My life was falling apart, and the few hours at a bar each night distracted me. Everyone acts so happy in a bar. The regulars seem the happiest, and I played the happiest regular. With each beer, my life crumbled a little more. Lies were piling up on more lies. "Life was good" was my biggest lie. The truth was my life sucked. Years later, my sister-in-law asked me if I wanted to die. "Hell Yeah!! Wouldn't you if you had my life?" Her silence spoke volumes. She would never say it, but I sensed she agreed with me.

In a few years, my marriage ended, my business failed, I lost the love of my life and the distance between myself and my family, including my kids, grew larger. My kids were the most important part of my life, and I couldn't take them seeing me crash and burn. I didn't even speak to any of my brothers or sisters. Old friends stayed away. Even the emptiness of my apartment was too much for me to deal with. But the bar always seemed to manufacture momentary happiness. Each moment gave us a reason to drink. A friend got a raise, or someone got laid off, ended with a raise of the glass. There were countless reasons to drink. Hot day? Drink. Rainy day? Drink. Snowstorm? Drink. Work sucked? Drink. Made a big sale? Drink. The list was never-ending. A brief thought of my pain would be forgotten with a quick sip of beer. Things were really bad.

Like an angel from heaven, this girl came into my life one day, and everything changed. Ironically, a song named "Angel" by Jon Secada was released around the same time we met. "I didn't wanna tell you things I didn't wanna know myself, but you gave me a reason to face the truth." Wow. The most amazing relationship I ever had begun at the perfect time. I always thought passion only occurred in sex. She taught me there was passion in everything. When the sun shined, and she smiled, my heart smiled too. I loved everything about her. The way she walked, the way she talked, the feel of her touch, the sweet words of encouragement, and her unpredictability, were all incredible. She restored my drive for everything I wanted; the most important thing I wanted was her. One time I remember us being out with a bunch of friends, and we were at opposite ends of all the conversations. From across the room, we looked into each other's eyes, and the electricity of our connection exploded. Even the friend I was talking to noticed it. "Would you two just go get a room?" I played it off, saying I was just looking around. But our eyes locked together all night, and I never felt closer to someone so far away.

In an instant, I lost her. She was my best friend and lover. More importantly, she was my reason to live; losing her meant I lost my spirit. My life went from hopeful to unbearable. I had no one. It didn't matter. No one could help me. My drinking got worse. I never wanted a drink. Honestly, I never did. I just wanted the pain to stop for a day. One day, I guess it was too much to ask for. I remember talking to my mom before she died. She asked me what I wanted. I told her I want to make it to "Day One." I meant I wanted to walk on a beach with my arm around the woman I loved and feel at peace. Now, the day was never gonna happen. Why live? It was a selfish question. My kids, family, and friends loved me, but I was lost in an ocean of misery. I couldn't feel their love, see the love, and didn't even care about their love. This was the real me, and the fake me hid the pain. I never once told a soul in the bar what was really happening because then I'd have to face it.

The punches kept coming. I lived a mile from my ex, and my father would visit her and my kids without telling or seeing me. A few years after my second son was born, my father pulled me aside and told me I would have to say something to my wife because "her ass was looking too big." I couldn't believe what I heard. I mean, she was my wife, and I loved her. So, after we split up, he visited her and my kids? Stealing happiness. What could my kids possibly think about what he was doing? I could only imagine them thinking, "Even his dad chose Mom over him. He must be terrible." Holidays would come and pass, and he'd be there, celebrating Christmas while his son was home alone year after year after year. Raising my kids, there was not one day I was drunk in front of them. But these horrible experiences lead me to drink more with each holiday. And every year had a lot of holidays. I would sit at the bar and think, *How could my dad do this?* No one knew, though. My smile always hid the pain. We all hide pain like it's something we're ashamed of.

I remember my health was starting to decline. My blood pressure was dangerously high (185/130), and I kept gaining weight. I had no health insurance. My mom was really worried and called my dad, a doctor, to find a good cardiologist in Baltimore for me to get examined. I felt unbearable stress. My dad decided to call my ex to find a cardiologist. Not me. Little did he know the doctor she recommended was the same doctor I found for her years earlier. I guess it was another reason for him to look like "Super Dad" in front of my ex. I felt completely humiliated. He never called me to ask me if I was okay. Sure Doctor Dad and his medical voice would talk to me as if I was a patient, but he never talked to me as a dad would talk to his son. He'd been through two divorces, so I figured he would understand what I was going through, but he didn't. He didn't care. His visits to my ex and kids continued.

I kept drinking.

Realizing the pain of divorce and this bizarre experience led me to put on weight. I never ate to satisfy a "depressed hunger." I ate to create physical distance between myself and the world. I felt like an emotional leper and could never bring a woman into my world. I craved love, a love that would save me. But If I loved again, I couldn't let the woman I care about become involved in this mess. Drinking till I was drunk and eating till I was sick protected me from even trying to find love.

I remember one time I had a crush on this girl. I knew she was nice. I didn't know anything else about her, but I could see the kindness in her eyes. I barely ever talked to her because it was a complete disaster each time I did. I was a complete idiot, and she was always polite. Our longest conversation lasted about a minute, and I could see her thoughts in her eyes, "If you could stop acting like a jerk and just be yourself, maybe I'd talk to you." That was the problem. I completely lost my sense of self. "Nobody will like me. Why would they? I even hate myself."

Love was really important. I had it once and desperately craved it again. I knew I wasn't strong enough. It saved me once, though. Losing it almost killed me, but I'd go for it again in a heartbeat. Then the reality of my life would destroy the desire. I never wanted a "one night kinda love," and I would drink to avoid the temptation. Emotions were something I couldn't share. Fooling myself, sometimes I would talk to women and always leave them feeling like "He's a nice guy who drinks way too much." These conversations allowed me to mask the loneliness. Would I ever find a girl like the love of my life again? Certainly not in a bar. After these one-night conversations, I'd drive home drunk and think about my love. Reviewing my life and the women I dated always left me thinking, *There's HER, and then there's everybody else.* I probably said it a thousand times, and each time, it meant more. To satisfy this feeling, I began to write a book called *Her*.

I was empty, lonely, and every other word you could use to describe the feeling of truly being alone. Nobody ever caught on, making me feel even more alone and insignificant. I saw a post my son put up in a chat room without him knowing. "My Dad is fat and lazy; if he died tomorrow, I wouldn't be upset." Knowing your kid doesn't care whether you're dead or alive is the hardest thing I ever had to hear. I discussed this with my ex and said he's obviously upset with me and that I should talk to him and work it out. She was against the idea because he would know we were reading his posts. In the interest of co-parenting, I went along with her wishes. I remember driving away thinking she'd talk to him in a heartbeat if he said the same thing about her. It didn't seem right, but I wasn't strong enough to fight. My car found its way to the bar, and my face changed from hell to heaven. Being the happiest regular was bullshit. The fake me took so much strength from me and my body. When your son doesn't care if you're dead, do you really wanna live? Drinking got worse. People in the bar would ask me how my kids were, and I would brag about them. I'd make up stories about holidays and project a happy world, knowing my kids were angry with me.

My marriage wasn't based on good communication. I never once said how I truly felt. I was completely responsible. For some reason, I always said what I thought would resolve the argument, not what I felt. Looking back, the truth was we weren't a good match. If I had worried more about the truths in my feelings and less about the longevity of my marriage, we would've only lasted about two years instead of thirteen. Lying about anything, including my feelings, dooms a marriage. I lied about my feelings and about drinking. If I've learned one thing, lying completely destroys a woman's trust; without it, you have nothing. We had nothing.

I couldn't be myself with my wife, so it made sense I couldn't talk to my kids either. I spent five years working in counseling adolescents, and I couldn't even talk to my kids. That's pathetic. I was blind to the fact that I had lost myself. And I became everything I despised. A man who couldn't communicate… just like my father. Wow. My mom, a therapist, was in awe of my communication skills, and I couldn't communicate with the two most important people in my life. I said it before. There were countless reasons to drink.

However, the one reason I had not to drink was my mother's death. I didn't feel anything and didn't want alcohol to make me feel less. My mom was my best friend. And the only person I could tell about some of my hell. I couldn't tell her everything because it would overwhelm her. In fact, I really didn't tell her much, but the sound of her voice gave me temporary comfort. I couldn't tell her about my drinking because she drank too much as well. And it was the worst-kept secret in my family. We all knew it, but we rarely talked about it. It just made me feel more alone. Her funeral was amazing, and it temporarily healed some of the dysfunction in my family. Everybody loved and talked to each other. I knew this made Mom happy. It was all she ever wanted. Looking back now, our short-lived love was enough to stop me from drinking. It wasn't to be, though. After the funeral, I returned home and went straight to the bar. It was just another reason to drink. Sitting at the bar, I drank my beer. After several hours of drinking, I finally acknowledged to myself that I had a problem. It didn't stop me. I didn't care. I just wanted the pain to go away. My mom's death brought more pain, and I remember hoping I would die soon. Suicide takes too much courage and energy. In a weird way, not having either only made me feel worse.

From the day my mom died, I dared death to take me. Nobody noticed I was drinking more because I was still the happiest regular in the bar. Soon, I began to notice the color of my eyes change. I noticed the yellow. Even that didn't make me stop. Liver failure stared me in the mirror, and I bought Visine eye drops. While my worry didn't stop my drinking, the eye drops gave me a false sense of security. If nobody noticed, I could keep drinking. I continued to punish myself for all the wrongs in my life.

Earlier in 2009, I made a New Year's resolution to lose sixty pounds. While it made no sense, this was the thing in my life that changed me. I always kept my resolutions. It seemed pretty simple. Give up beer and fast food, and the weight would drop off. I even began to exercise. Thankfully, there weren't any withdrawal side effects. After a month of losing weight, mysteriously, it began to return. I convinced myself the swelling in my legs was muscle. This swelling got so bad that I couldn't bend at the knee. Shortness of breath followed. I continued working. Finally, I realized something was wrong when it took forty-five minutes to get out of my bed and walk a hundred feet to my car.

Driving myself to the hospital, I worried because I had no insurance. Hopefully, a prescription would make me all better. Four hours in an examination room and hundreds of tests scared me in a calming way because I began to accept that change HAD to happen. The doctor must've come in the room ten times to check out different symptoms. Each time, she became less friendly and more serious. I asked a million questions, and each one was met with a request for me to be patient. It seemed like she had hoped the blood tests were wrong until the fourth re-test confirmed the truth she dreaded telling me.

She entered my room and told me to sit down. "You keep doing what you're doing, and you'll be dead in two months. You must stop drinking immediately and change your eating habits."

My answer was simple. "Okay." I even felt a sense of relief.

The next day, I went to see my first specialist. "Tell me about your drinking."

One thought ran through my head. *If I'm lying, I'm dying.* I told him the complete truth. Again, I felt another sense of relief. After finishing my story, he said the most important statement in my life. "Well, John, listening to you, it seems like you've closed that chapter in your life." It was exactly what I needed to hear, and he was right. I was ready to start a new chapter. He gave me a prescription for diuretics to remove the fluid, and I went on my way. Walking to my car, I accepted the challenge that lay ahead. My mom battled cancer, and my goal was to be half as strong as she, and I knew I'd be okay.

Changes kept coming. The next day, I invited my friend Lynne over, and we began talking. In a second, my world fell apart as I confessed to her that my whole life was a complete lie. Crying so hard I couldn't stop or catch my breath. She was shaken to see me so broken and asked why I had never told her. Fighting through the sobbing tears, I said, "I didn't want you to think less of me." She responded in the most caring voice, "John,

I think more of you for being so honest." Those words saved my life, and I'll be forever indebted to my dear friend, Lynne.

Weekly visits with the doctor became monthly, and then monthly became quarterly. I started to believe I'd be okay. That bubble burst quickly. The fluid was called ascites and having it removed proved statistically risky. 50% of patients didn't last two years. Becoming educated about my symptoms only leads to constant reminders of the overwhelming odds. Dealing with these, I created an ironic boring routine. Thoughts of "OMG, I'm screwed" turned into days of processing the information, finding a resolution with determination to fight to live, sprinkled with "who cares, that isn't going to happen to me" I've learned to live life like no one else. "Laugh, Think and Cry" every day, and Jim Valvano was right. It is pretty special. Now I laugh like it tickles and cry like it hurts. Both feel good.

On January 3rd, 2010, I met with 12 doctors from the transplant team at Penn. In a conference room, I sat in the middle of them, and the chief of the transplant team was the only one who spoke and had one question. "Why should we do a transplant on you?"

I took a deep breath and spoke with a passion I never knew I had about why I deserved one over others. I guaranteed them I would make it to the operating room table; after that, it was their turn to do the rest. It worked. He said, "Normally, we all meet, but you convinced me you were deserving, and I'm sure my team would agree." I saw a lot of nodding in the room. My sense of relief was short-lived. I learned I would have to get a lot sicker before they could do anything. That sucked!

The medical consequences of alcohol abuse are overwhelming, and my purpose is to make people aware of them. People who ask me how much I drank don't like my answer. They ask because they want to know if they should worry about themselves or a loved one. "However much I drank, my body decided it was too much." My bloodwork was decent six months before I was given two months to live. Your body says enough's enough at any time. My biggest concern is people think it will never happen to them. I've realized nothing will make a person stop drinking until they want to stop. I saw fourteen people die of cirrhosis. I'm the only one I know of that lived.

One of the medicines I had to take three times a day was called lactulose. This is a powerful laxative that removes the toxins that the liver can't clean. One day Lynne's daughter went into labor. I stayed by her side and drove her to the hospital, where she gave birth to a gift in my life, Christina. After she was born, I had to drive nine hours through West Virginia. I hadn't taken my medicine in thirty hours. The people in West Virginia were terrible drivers!!! I kept hearing people honking their horns. When I finally got to my hotel, I went right to bed. I woke up to a phone call from a friend who immediately noticed something was wrong. She asked for my brother's phone number, and I couldn't find it. She then asked me, "What's your brother's name?" I replied that I didn't know. She asked me, "John, what's your name?" Again, I replied that I didn't know. She told me she was calling my doctor immediately. They found a pharmacy right by the hotel, and I got my lactulose. An hour later, I went to the bathroom, and all the toxins were removed from my body. Unbeknownst to me, I had hepatic encephalopathy. Basically, it means I hallucinated because the toxins went to my brain, and I had been driving with this!!! I'll never be able to understand how I was still alive. I do know that I was incredibly lucky and learned I had to be 100% compliant with my medications.

Early in my battle with cirrhosis, I had twenty liters of fluid drained from my stomach each week. The doctor recommended I have a procedure called T.I.P.S. It stands for TransJugular Intrahepatic Stent. This procedure reduced the fluid from twenty liters a week to about six liters once a month.

Six years ago, I woke up in Shock Trauma after five days of being on life support. And there was Shari, my partner, holding my hand. The doctor immediately came in to assess me. Shari's mom was sitting beside her, and I noticed her. I made a typical mother-in-law face that made Shari and her mom laugh and say, "That's the John we know and love!!" Even the doctor laughed. I was going to be okay. I was in the hospital for about a month.

May 2020 was a wild month. I had stomach pain and went to the doctor. Healthwise, I was so good that I was taken off the transplant list because I was too healthy. My MELD score was 7. (To get a transplant, you have to be about 30.) My doctor decided to do a procedure, and my MELD jumped to a 15. A few days later, the procedure was repeated, and it jumped to a 22. Then they brought a specialist in to do it, and I woke up, and my MELD was a 28. I was going to Philadelphia to get a transplant. While I was scared and confused because I didn't feel I was at death's door, I was very excited. This occurred during the Philadelphia riots and the beginning of covid restrictions. Shari, my rock, was not allowed to go. I arrived on a Friday night and was met by one of the doctors on the transplant team. She told me they were 100% confident this was a good match, and I responded, "I'm 100% confident in you. Let's do this!"

The harsh reality of transplant is someone has to die for you to live. Live with that one for a minute or two. It's not fun. Consumed in thought about this, I received a phone call from Mark. I coached Mark in several sports from the time he was seven. He was now thirty and called to wish me good luck. I heard a lot of concern in his voice and asked him what was wrong. "Coach John, I just don't want you to die." I downplayed the seriousness of the operation and promised him I would call him tomorrow after the surgery, and he knew I kept my promises.

Game Day!!

I waited twelve years for this day. As they came in to take my stretcher to the operating room, I smiled and said, "Let's do this." It became my mantra.

The surgeon came by to check on me outside the operating room. I had to ask him, "You remember what I said ten years ago?"

He responded with confidence, "Yes, I do, John. It's my turn now." That's all I needed to hear!!! I couldn't believe he remembered my guarantee.

The operating room is like a rock concert. The big stars are the last to come in. The nursing staff greeted me as I was wheeled in. They were fired up! One asked me what music I wanted to hear, and I told them "Thunder Road " by Bruce Springsteen. Literally, the whole team sang the song with me. It was an amazing moment. Next, we heard "Born to Run," and I broke down in tears because the first verse was my high school senior quote. "Baby, this town rips the bones from your back. It's a death trap, suicide rap. We got to get out while we're young." My parents had been going through an ugly divorce, and this time was the start of my drinking to escape my reality. Luckily for me, the anesthesiologist gave me the medicine to put me under. The operation took a total of 18 hours. And it was an amazing success.

The anesthesia wore off, and I woke up to ice packs on my stomach. While I was out of it, I couldn't believe the limited amount of pain I felt. I didn't need pain medication. The first thing I did was call Shari; her voice was music to me. It was great to hear the relief in her voice. I put her through hell for years, and that was in the rearview mirror. I didn't have any complications. However, before the transplant, I would always sit down to pee because of the constant fatigue. I took advantage of any chance to rest! Well, twenty-four hours after surgery, I had to go, and I used my walker to get to the bathroom. I can't explain why but I stood up to pee and literally laughed out loud. Life was getting back to normal, and it felt great.

Day eight was discharge day! Again because of covid, Shari was not allowed in the hospital, but she was parked right outside the entrance. I was wheeled to the passenger car door, stood up, and got in. It felt amazing to hug Shari. I didn't feel any pain. Love is the best painkiller!! Driving away, Penn was in the rear-view mirror, literally and figuratively. I had mixed emotions. Penn was a place that would give hope to so many people in the same boat as me.

I remember striking up a conversation with a woman on the transplant list. She asked me what I wanted to be remembered for. I thought for a minute and told her, "I want to be remembered for loving and accepting everyone for exactly who they are and maybe making them laugh a little." I was convinced my answer sounded really good.

Then she shocked me with her response. "Are you living that way?"

I was stunned and forced to think about it. I responded, "I don't know." I know I sounded distressed.

With an encouraging voice, she replied, "Why don't you try?" It was a life-changing moment for me. And today, I try to keep that commitment.

While being diagnosed with cirrhosis has been one of the worst things that ever happened (it took me six months even to say the word), it was also the best. Cirrhosis gave me a new life that I treasure every day. I'm a completely different person now. I love more, laugh harder, and live better than I ever have before. Even with the tough days, I wouldn't trade this experience for anything. When you're faced with a life-threatening illness, you have a decision to make. You must decide how you want to live and how you want to be remembered. I promise you that a positive perspective is a beautiful thing. The last words before my mom died were, "Positive Thoughts." She taught me a lesson with those words that saved my life. Today life is a gift, and I treasure each day.

As far as my past life, I recently found a quote from *Alice in Wonderland* that best describes how I feel. "But that was yesterday; I was a different person then."

John Weiman

John was the fifth child in a family of five. As an adult, he used to say, with a smile, his mom was five for nine in pregnancies. He was 42 years old before he realized he was the ninth pregnancy. It overwhelmed him to think about the pain his mother went through to have him. To family members and close friends, he was called Johno.

As a kid, he loved riding his bicycle and rode it all over the busy streets of New York. At ten years old, he took his courage too far and got hit by a car. He suffered a bad concussion and spent the night in the hospital. He assured his mom and dad that he was old enough to spend the night alone in the hospital. The courage was short-lived, and he called his mother to return to the hospital. He credits his mother for being the man he is today.

Childhood was full of games of hide and seek, capture the flag, legendary games of basketball, and a love for boating.

He continues to have that love today when he and his wife live on The Chesapeake Bay and spend their time in their Carver boat. Their dream is to do The Great Loop, which is a 6000-mile journey around the waters of the United States.

John is one of the highest-rated marriage counselors in the country and loves his job. He has created a model where the sessions are not limited to a clock. He wants couples to walk out better than they walked in. He proudly says the record is five hours and fifteen minutes.

He's proud of how he's taken lemons and made them lemonade!

https://lifebridgecoaching.com/
(410) 419-8149

It's All About the Packaging

By Jeanne Perkins

As I enter my 55th year, I reflect on how I took challenges and transformed them into sweet success. I am in a deep transformational phase of my life which is having me redefine my career, my core values, who I am, and what my purpose is. My entire professional life focused on creating packaging for top fragrance companies creating beauty. It left me yearning for something deeper, more meaningful, and fulfilling; now, I am focusing on the most important package - me!

Dad always told me packaging was everything.

My father owned a printing company in New York City (NYC). As a child, I spent numerous nights and weekends erasing small marks on papers and collating printing jobs. It became a family affair. My father wrapped up each printing job with special care. He said that if the outer package was perfect, there was never a rejection. My father's printing shop was a small business downtown near Chinatown. He had many accounts that included museums, colleges, well-known businesses, and famous restaurants; all the business came through word of mouth. My father had an amazing work ethic and was kind and generous; clients loved working with him because he was reliable. My father worked hard and was very dedicated to his family. I held the same work ethic all my life because that is what I saw from my father. He prided himself on the fact that he never missed a day of work, even when he was sick. He even had perfect attendance in High School! Now at this stage in my life, it is about not working harder but working smarter so I can enjoy my family and life.

New York City was always about success.

NYC has fascinated me since I was a young child growing up in a small suburb in New Jersey. My father had his printing business, and my uncle had a movie theater and candy store in the Bronx. My grandmother took me to NYC by bus all the time. She was my biggest cheerleader. My grandmother believed in me. She died right before I turned 17, but before passing, she told my aunt/godmother to ensure that I went to college no matter what. I loved NYC, and there was no question in my mind that I would be working and living in NYC when I grew up. It was mysterious, sexy, lively, and full of energy! One of my childhood friends recently said, "Jeanne, you were always New York even before you were New York." I took this as a huge compliment. As the saying goes, "if you can make it there, you can make it anywhere."

I started my career by accident!

I stumbled upon my first job in the Fragrance and Cosmetic industry by finding a $20 bill outside an office building in NYC. I was interviewing for weeks and was tired of going to headhunter agencies when I thought they were the actual company. When I arrived for one interview, the elevator wasn't working, and I had to go to the freight elevator. An elevator operator told me he would take me to the agency. When I realized it was another agency, I turned around to leave and found $20 on the sidewalk. I thought to myself, "Hmmm, it might be my lucky day." I went into the agency after all, and they sent me directly to the company for an interview. I got the job on the spot! This day would start my 30 years in packaging within the fragrance and cosmetic industry. My position allowed me to work and travel around the United States, Europe, and Asia. I worked for manufacturers all over the globe, including France, Germany, Spain, the UK, China, Hong Kong, as well as the United States. My eye for detail, which I learned as a child from helping my father with the printing jobs, was in full use. I helped create beautiful packages for almost every major fragrance company in the industry. I became an expert in sales for packaging using many different types of materials and processes. Every element was so important to fit together and be esthetically elegant. Dad was right; it was all about the PACKAGING!

Pivoting at the right time changes everything.

My career wasn't always rosy. Early in my career, I worked for a European company and ran the U.S. office. The company purchased one of our competitors domestically and merged the two companies. I was very successful in my area, which focused primarily on metal packaging, and my competitor, now a colleague, was successful in plastic packaging. How would this newly merged company work? Could we make it as Co-Presidents? We were competitive, and our working styles were different. After a short time, I decided to give up my title of President and focus on what I was good at - Sales! At the time, major companies like Estée Lauder were just starting to talk about manufacturing in China. My younger brother was doing a summer program in China for his Master's degree. China was becoming a theme, and I thought, "China is a new area I don't know much about. Let me jump in!"

Knowing my worth allowed me great opportunities.

I applied for a job at a small Hong Kong Chinese company, and the interview was in the tea room at the Plaza Hotel in NYC. As I walked into the Plaza Tea room, I knew my life was about to change. They offered me the option of a salary or a commission. I knew my impressive skill set, so I took the commission-only option. This company gave me a small draw versus commission and said we could reconcile after six months. I responded, "if I owe you money in six months, there is a big issue for both of us." I was young, aggressive, and very confident. I worked 20-hour days between the team in China and the customers in the U.S. I took the company to the next level; there was no stopping me because there was no limit. When the company grew exponentially, and they wanted to sell to a big Chinese firm, they were forced to put in structure. They eliminated my commission, and it happened the very same week that I was getting separated from my marriage. They hired my former co-president as my boss! At this point, I had "golden handcuffs." I was getting paid slightly above anywhere else I could go but much lower than my unlimited commission had been. I kept my head down and continued to work. It was not easy because I was a newly single mom in NYC. Despite the setbacks, I was their top producer. I was comfortable, making good money, in a job that was easy for me because of my experience. But I had this yearning for something more rewarding, more challenging. Something I could build on my own. I was making a good salary, and I was successful at what I did, so the thought of burning the boat and starting a new career was difficult. The people closest to me said I was crazy to do anything else.

When is the right time to exit?

When working for this corporation, there was always that concern of being at the top of the cake when it was going to be cut. There were many changes throughout the years, but I managed to stay. Once COVID happened, there were talks about the uncertainty of the company. I listened carefully to the meetings and volunteered for a pay cut for six months. Shortly after, it was mandatory for everyone anyway, but you were favorably considered if you had volunteered. Whew, I made the cut! There were constant layoffs all around me. Instead of being laid off, they told me they would reduce my salary in 6 months. They said, "We are overpaying you." I couldn't help but think, "WHAT?!" I was forced to think about Plan B. "What can I do? What will I do? I have been at this company for 18 years. Could I possibly go to a competitor and repackage myself?"

My son has always been my biggest teacher.

A series of events led me to go to China, and I returned exhausted. My husband and I decided to book a trip to St. Barts to rest and regenerate. I woke up in St Barts the first morning with six kittens on the doorstep. Was this some sign? Indeed, I had conceived. A beautiful baby boy who has enriched my life in a way I never thought possible.I ended up getting a divorce when my son was around five years old. When my son was seven years old, we talked about the days of the week. He said, "Mommy, there is no tomorrow!" I said, "Of course, there is a tomorrow." He then said, "LIFE is just one continuous day, and there is no separation between today and tomorrow." This blew me away! Here I was just starting to grasp the concept of "LIVING IN THE MOMENT," but my son had just explained to me how to be in the moment and that life is just one big, long day, so make it count. I was in my 40s, and my life focus started to be on spiritual expansion. I started to dive deep into different trainings for energetic healing modalities as a hobby as I was already successful in the packaging business.

The Healing Journey

Looking back, my journey in the healing arts started when I was very young. When I was a little girl, my grandfather would sit me on his lap and tell me that someday he wouldn't be here. He was preparing me for his death. I didn't understand what he was saying until he passed away when I was 13. His passing was the first death I experienced. But where did he go? I became obsessed with researching life after death. I would go to the local library and take out every book I could. I started to teach myself how to connect to the other side during my dream state. These connections strengthened when I went to college, and my visions became much stronger. I was drawn to the metaphysical section in bookstores, which fueled my passion for learning and developing my intuition and energetic skillset. I believe in signs from the universe. I have learned to follow up on my instincts and not to give up.

As my hobby grew in the metaphysical world, I opened a wellness center in NYC with my new husband. I launched my first side hustle called the Genie Pod, a machine using heat and light healing therapy. I kept this service going for a few years but then started to utilize my healing modalities, limiting them to helping family, friends, and random strangers that would consistently pop up in the craziest situations. I started to hear and see amazing results. My training includes Vortex Healing, John Newton's ancestral clearing, Damien Wynn's Light Grids, Naam Yoga Harmonyum practitioner, Garcia Energetics, and Raymon Grace dowsing technique, to name a few.

For example, I was in Columbus on business heading back to Newark airport (NYC). This flight is always late, with usually only a few people on the plane. Before boarding, the seat next to me was empty. After I sat down, a frantic woman sat in the empty seat by me. I was thinking to myself, no one should be sitting here. This woman was in her 40s and explained that she never traveled alone because of panic attacks, especially traveling to Newark airport. She said she couldn't understand why she was in such a panic and looked around. Everyone else was calm. I feel my inner guidance urging me to help her. Finally, I asked her if she was open for me to help her with her panic attacks regarding flying. She said she would wait until it was full-blown. But I insisted that we not wait. I held a safe space for her, and within minutes, we discovered that when she was five years old, she witnessed a fight between her parents, and her mother said she didn't want to be a mother anymore. It was the last time she saw her. Her father was stationed in Europe then, so she was put on a plane to Newark by herself and experienced extreme turbulence as they approached the runway. She was crying hysterically. This memory was lodged in her nervous system, causing havoc in her adult life. As she safely witnessed this, she emailed me the next day saying her life was transformed and she felt like dancing when getting off the plane.

Once, my relative was getting knee surgery, and nothing was giving him relief for his knee. We discovered in minutes that when he was a child, he was on a swing set, having a great time when the entire swing set collapsed, and he hurt his knee. This trauma has been trapped in his knee for decades. He gently witnessed this experience, and now the deep healing on his knee could begin.

During Covid, I helped rebrand and relaunch the wellness center in Flatiron, NY. I still work with people to instantly change the energetic dynamic of their family and intimate relationships. I have watched people I work with suddenly create harmonious relationships and/or meet incredible partners.

Losing My Father

Two years before my father passed away, I had panic attacks waking up in the night feeling that I had lost my jewelry. I would jump up, yell, and check my wrists and fingers to see if my jewelry was missing. I started to have breathing issues, so I went to my father's internist, and they did an asthma test. I was negative for asthma, but the doctor put me on inhalers anyway. It didn't make sense.

Two weeks before he passed away, I took my father to his doctor. He hadn't been feeling well and I was anxious to get him checked out.. They couldn't find anything more than the high blood pressure I knew he had my entire life. They sent me across the hall to the neurologist. Because of insurance issues, the thanksgiving holiday, and scheduling, the best available appointment was seven days past the holiday. I knew something was wrong. I kept calling the doctor to see if they could get him seen sooner, but they were busy with the holiday. My parents planned a trip to Florida for Thanksgiving to visit relatives, so I thought he would go to Florida, relax, and go to the doctor when he returned. But my father never returned.

I went to sleep Sunday night after Thanksgiving watching a special on TV about Natalie Wood and her tragic death. What struck me the most was listening to her daughters say that the one thing they missed the most was calling someone mom. I went to bed with this heavy thought on my mind. The next thing I knew, I had a vision of my dad walking toward the light while I was in a dream state in the early morning hours. My inner voice told my father, "go to the light, go to the light." Then I realized what I was saying, so I yelled, "NO, NO, NO!" Ten minutes later, while I was still asleep, my mother called. I jumped out of bed screaming like the panic attacks I'd had for two years prior. My mother said, "Daddy is dead." It was a heart attack while they were at the airport gate heading back home.

He had spent that weekend at Universal Studios with my relatives. One of the last photos I saw of him was wearing a red American Heart Association hat that my uncle let him wear that day. In the photo, my father's face was swollen; I could see something terribly wrong even through his smiles. Oh my, there were signs everywhere! Why didn't anyone see them? This photo was taken under the Jaws shark by the man-made pier at Universal Studios. My father died at the Orlando airport a few months before they launched defibrillators at the airports. The doctors said there was no chance of saving him without one.

I had an aversion to even going to the state of Florida after that. It was so bad that when my friends invited me to visit, they took me to Bimini in the Bahamas on their boat, so I didn't have to stay in Florida physically.

About ten years later, when my son was young, we went on a Disney cruise out of Cape Canaveral. I decided to stay an extra few days. I wanted to turn this around. I took the most difficult emotional feeling about Universal Studios and decided to take my son there. I walked through the park, went on the rides, and stood in line. I imagined every moment my father experienced in the park and how he might have felt on that day . I wondered which rides he went on. He did not know it would be his last day on earth. My visit was extremely bittersweet.

Universal Studios became an extraordinary place to take my son on our annual special vacations. We went every year. We just went a few months ago when he was 17 years old. We had the best time, but it's very different than when he was young. I don't do rollercoasters, but I forced myself to be brave and push past my comfort zone. In general, I always lean towards pushing my edges for growth. Losing my father is the biggest heartbreak I have had in my life. I felt all my security disappear in one split second. Life will never be the same. It has been over 20 years now. Although my father did not support me financially, I was 30 years old and felt a huge loss of security in all areas of my life, including finances.

Leaning into new skills.

I remembered what my son said one day when I asked him what he wanted to be when he grew up. As we drove down the highway, he said, "I want to learn real estate from you, Mom." That thought motivated me to learn everything I could about real estate investing and becoming an entrepreneur. I did not look at myself as a real estate investor, but I started to dabble in training and discovered a faith-based woman's real estate investing network based out of Dallas, Texas. I immersed myself in the program, but then COVID hit. I had difficulty keeping up with the training as we were closing the wellness center in NYC at the time and deciding how to prepackage, rebrand and reopen.

My real estate mentor would always say, you are not a real estate investor unless you are marketing. I launched my first marketing campaign in August of 2022. Randomly, I received a phone call the next day. My company stated that my position of 19 years has been eliminated, effective immediately! Two days later,

I received my first verbal real estate contract from the marketing campaign I had just launched.

There is a lot of uncertainty in not knowing your destination. There are bumps, turns, and delays, but ultimately, I trust this will lead me to discover who I am and what my purpose is. I know that there is always a solution and always a way. The real estate group I am in focuses on becoming strong and fearless. I want to teach this to my son as I build a real estate legacy for him.

Now I am getting my juice back. I am networking and making new connections. I am growing my business day by day and expanding my knowledge while focusing on what I am good at, which is finding solutions. My energetic practices, strong sales and negotiation experience, and specialized real estate knowledge allow me to help homeowners in difficult situations find winning solutions.

I purchased my first property in Sedona, Arizona. The house was already an Alice in Wonderland-themed Airbnb. It is magical for all that come, and this has been part of my journey. I started to discover there is more to reality than meets the eye. My outer world was about packaging, but my inner world was a mixture of the seen and unseen world. I went down my own rabbit hole as I started taking tantra classes and woman empowerment courses and joined quite a few powerful women's support groups. Like Alice, I was searching for my identity, giving up old comforts and taking on new challenges while working through all the moments of anxiety and confusion. I am thankful for the many teachers and mentors who helped me along the way.

I am trying to follow a path of self-discovery and curiosity as Alice did. Nothing is as it appears; light is not just light, and time is relative. If life is an illusion and time doesn't matter, is this what my son was trying to teach me when he was a child?

My Superpower

I grew up extremely shy as a child. I would barely speak to anyone, especially men, as I was terrified of them. I wouldn't even speak to my male relatives. Only my father and grandfather made me feel safe. It was difficult for my parents to find a woman dentist to take care of my teeth. It happened to be with the first woman dentist in New Jersey. It was so expensive for them that they could barely afford it. I couldn't even go to the local shoe store and get measured for shoes. I'm not sure exactly when I grew out of this shyness, but it was around the time I started to like boys. Communication as a child was always difficult for me. I struggled to express my needs even to my parents and grandparents.

When I entered adulthood, I took this communication challenge and became a top salesperson in the fragrance industry. Some people would call me the Michael Jordan of the industry. Communication became my focus. I became trained in NLP (neurolinguistic programming), developed active listening skills, and used my intuition to be at the right place at the right time with the right information. I grew up from this shy little girl from New Jersey to a New York City power executive.

Every setback, rejection, firing, and breakup is tough for me, but I allow myself to feel all my emotions. I have a toolbox of techniques to help me through the process, whether it's body movement, talking, tapping, or mindset work, among many others. After processing, I can always find the silver lining. Whether it be a project that I was denied at work, my son's rejection letter from a college, or my relationship breakups, this allows me to see what no longer serves me. How many times have I repackaged myself? I keep having to do it over and over as a single mom, wife, investor, student, teacher, energy facilitator, executive, and terrified little girl. I must recreate again a stronger, better me with more direction. It is an opportunity to repackage myself and make lemonade again. Packaging is about intentional care. It is not about perfection; that, is not what it is about. Packaging is about how you look and feel about something in its best light. It is about overcoming all of life's challenges of the past and creating beauty out of chaos. For me, it is picking up all my loose pieces and making the best life possible, inside and out. I am still growing daily, recreating myself in the process.

My communication and repackaging skills became my superpowers and made me great at networking and connecting people for their success. Now my challenge is to do this for myself! How does one reinvent the most important package? Creating beauty in one form or another has been my passion. What can be done to overcome and create beauty through my own transformation and through helping others?

My word for this year is Freedom.

I freed myself from self-imposed prisons, and now I am pushing towards consistency and persistence toward my goals. I use every day as an opportunity to enjoy myself, make someone happy, or grow. I do it all in my uniquely packaged way. I am working on finding a balance between the warrior and the lover. There are always challenges and difficulties in life, but I am confident there is always a solution. I transformed myself from this shy little girl to a now former New York power executive, so I already have the evidence that this can be done, and now I can transform into whatever I want to create next.

My advice is never to give up. Just keep squeezing those lemons, and be sure to use the peel to zest the top.

Jeanne Perkins

Jeanne is a lover of life. She looks at every situation as an opportunity to grow, connect with people or share her love of learning. She was born in NJ as a shy little girl, who overcame huge obstacles to become a fragrance and beauty product packaing executive in NYC. She has travelled all over the world for business and pleasure and recently redefined herself as a healer and real estate investor. She is constantly looking at ways to improve her life be it through healing modalities, taking classes or giving herself challenges that most would not consider possible. For her most recent birthday, she challenged herself to climb up one of NYC's highest outdoor challenges, The City Climb, a edgy building in Hudson Yards where she dangled over the side of the building! She is not afraid to push her edges to look at life straight on and say YES!

To contact Jeanne: Jeannejayperkins@gmail.com

Living The Sweet Life – The RV Edition

by Laura Ann Garris

The year 2020 was one of the most difficult years of my life. Nothing made sense anymore. Everything needed a fresh reframe and extra love for me to continue forward. I did not know how much I had left to give to that year's holiday season, but I had made up my mind. I was going to give it and my family every ounce of faith, honor, and intrepid compassion I had left in me!

South Carolina became a new focal point for our Seattle family in 2020. My teenage daughter, Ella, had decided to relocate there with her beloved grandmother after a summer visit. Her new home seemed to provide the relief she sought from the months of migraines, depression, and hopelessness stemming from the pandemic lockdowns. South Carolina's openness and ability to hang out with her grandmother seemed to be the salve that her soul needed. Still, there was a catch that developed from the relocation. Ella had to return to Seattle and finish her six-week driver's ed course to get her driver's license.

Finally, with the course finished and the license in hand, she was ready to return to South Carolina, fully independent. But how was I going to let her go and say goodbye? I did not want to walk her to security at the airport and drop her off. That felt too harsh, like a gash down my heart that would never stop bleeding.

No, I wanted to savor this. I wanted one last family adventure. My son was about to graduate high school in June, and if he was off to college, we would not be together again for a long time. This was the end of the "childhood years." Now a young woman and man, my children were nearly grown. What would I do with this precious ending of a life chapter?

One of our family's favorite movies is *RV* with Robin Williams. This classic comedy showed the family coming together through the highs and lows of an adventurous RV trip. With each family member enduring their trip with patience, love, and a sense of humor, they ultimately built a stronger and more resilient bond than ever. When I thought of how I wanted to end 2020, this was the image I had in my mind.

Since I was already getting the last two weeks of December off, I had an idea. I would take an additional two weeks off and spend one month with my family and our two German Shepherds, driving roundtrip from Seattle to South Carolina in our RV, racking up a total of 7000 miles. Didn't that sound like fun?

My husband thought I was crazy, especially since he knew he would be doing most of the driving, but he listened. We both slept on the idea. The next morning, he agreed with me. It was the perfect time for a road trip adventure. We would be able to see friends and both of our parents and be self-contained with food, toilet, and sleeping accommodations. I leaped for joy and then went to work creating the family adventure of my dreams, and as I should have realized by now, nothing ever went according to plan.

As I considered the upcoming holiday trip, I thought of the usual way things would get done. In my home, I was the one who decorated and brought the celebration to each holiday. When the Christmas tree box appeared, my entire family magically fled to the far corners of the house with other things to do. It was almost like they were all draped in a magical invisibility cloak, nowhere to be found. Now on this RV trip, they would have nowhere to escape. I would have them within 35 feet of me for the two weeks before Christmas. It was the perfect excuse to revamp Christmas magic *and* bring out a little extra celebratory joy.

"...We rejoice in our *sufferings*, knowing that *suffering* produces *endurance*, and e*ndurance* produces *character*, and *character* produces *hope,* and *hope* does not disappoint us, because God's love has been poured into our hearts through the Holy Spirit that has been given to us." Romans 5:3-5

The first thing I did was find items for the "12 Days of Christmas—RV Style." I would surprise them daily with a gift, activity, or event. Then, sing a humorous rendition of the "12 Days of Christmas" song while presenting it to them.

It went like this:

On the first day of *"our Christmas RV Road Trip,"* my parents gave to me...

Some comic books and origami...

Okay, this was not the highlight of the twelve gifts, but it set the tone. My teenagers rolled their eyes at the goofy, silly items. We all laughed as I stood there, singing in my wild Christmas sweater and two dogs barking beside me in harmony. There was nowhere to go, so they browsed through their books, wondering what tomorrow might bring.

We all needed some lightness. 2020 had some heavy moments. We were still grieving our dear neighbor, who had been a father of three, grandfather of two, and a beloved husband. He took his own life in May.

My son, Jack, had been outside playing basketball when he heard the shot. He quickly ran from our backyard over the neighbor's fence to see our neighbor's son pulling his hysterical mother out through the front door. Immediately fire engines, police cars, and ambulances arrived on the scene as our street was closed with an intricate web of yellow crime scene tape.

As we ran out to find out what happened, our neighbor's wife sat in the driveway, facing our home, wailing, lamenting, and screaming for her husband. The family was trying to comfort her to no avail. It was a sight and sound that shook your very soul. A moment of rawness and complete vulnerability connected us all to the loss of a world that no longer made sense.

I had to do something, anything at all! I had to let them know we cared; we loved them. They were not alone in this Hell. So, my husband and I crossed the police tape. Screw the Covid mandate, screw the masks, and no touching. We walked up to the three grieving sons and hugged them mightily. The young men wept, and we wept along with them. Their dad was gone. He had taken his own life in his own house while his wife and son were in the kitchen.

The loud wailing heartache of his wife went on into the early morning hours. I took her cries deep into my heart. It was like a million nails raking into my soul. Her beloved was dead. The preciousness of life is so short. Covid was killing thousands this year. The lockdowns, mandates, isolation, suicides, depression, addictions, and fear were doing so much more. They were maiming us for the long term—creating families without fathers, youth without hope, and neighbors afraid to touch each other when we needed them the most.

The neighborhood felt like a cesspool of grief for the next few days. Trauma still lingered in the air. The remaining neighbors came together and prayed for the family. We listened to each other with deep compassionate hearts and cried as we shared stories of past joyful neighborhood memories. Life would continue even through the tears.

On the second day of "our Christmas RV Road Trip," my parents gave to me …

Some Cinnabon Rolls and a latte….

December 13th was St. Lucia Day in Sweden with its fun traditions of cinnamon braided pastries in honor of its patron. My family was blessed to have lived in northern Sweden during 2009-2010 when the children were small. My daughter, with all the other preschool girls, were dressed up as St. Lucia. They had battery-operated candles in their hair and wore white dresses as they entered the local Lutheran church service. Today, I served my family Cinnabon Rolls dripping with icing, recalling the whimsical memories of Sweden and the traditions of the Arctic North. The Cinnabon Rolls were devoured within minutes alongside the smiles and laughter of years gone by as they returned to their devices and headsets as we traveled through the endless miles of highways.

Later on, we pulled off onto a dirt road in the high desert area of Arizona called Devil's Dog Road to spend the night. It was a clear night with no light pollution. As the Geminid meteor shower fell, the clear brilliance of the stars and planets gave me goosebump chills. It definitely lived up to its prediction as "the best meteor shower of 2020."

We all stood outside in the pitch-black night, watching this historic meteor shower whiz by us, huddling together for warmth. A moment of complete awe. A perfect moment that I knew I would savor over and over again. There were just the four of us, with the stars and the endless possibilities of what was to come as we felt enveloped in a love greater than any of us.

This life was full of miracles. I recounted how faithful God had been to us this year. My husband, at 54, had been laid off from his company in December 2019. As soon as we found out, we prayed together that God would send him the perfect position soon and protect our family during this transition. Then, we decided to go out that night and celebrate with a great dinner and live music, trusting on faith alone that all would be provided.

A month passed, and thanks to a lead from a friend, he landed a great senior-level position at a new job that allowed for high-earning potential and travel throughout the Pacific Northwest. In February 2020, our prayers had been answered. We would be financially okay, no matter what came our way.

On the third day of "our Christmas RV Road Trip," my parents gave to me…

Santa suit onesies and caroling…

My son went through so much that year. His senior year in high school was a train wreck, full of closed opportunities and isolation, and he was denied his cherished baseball. In January 2020, he had been rear-ended by an uninsured motorist while at a four-way stop, which gave him a major concussion. He had been forced to stay at home to rest, which caused him to sit out the first two weeks of baseball in March. And then the unthinkable happened—lockdown and no baseball. He had his dreams dashed, and his spirit went along with it. Today, however, was his 18th birthday, and I had a special gift for him—MATCHING SANTA ONESIES!

As we made it into the Phoenix area and my mother's home, I pulled out the Santa suits and began to sing "On the Third Day of Our Christmas…" My son's face was panic-stricken. He did not think this was going to be fun. AND WHAT… he had to SING! He put his foot down. That was not going to happen.

After much persuasion and a little bribery from my husband and me, my son put on his Santa suit and sang with us in an outstanding performance for my mom and her neighbors. Everyone laughed and joked. My mom took a photo of my family, capturing the boldness of us in the Santa suits. It is still my favorite holiday photo of the entire trip. This day became a turning point for my kids when they realized that these "12 Days of Christmas" gifts WERE happening and they should just lean into it and have some fun!

Now, I had to search for something that might seem cool for my son. I promised we would get out of the geriatric wonderland and let him have time to do what he wanted. At last, we found Cow Town. It was one of the original skateboard shops with a public skateboard park. Though it was located across town, we checked it out anyway. He bought some items, and the guys working there called his custom skateboard *"gnarly."* It made his day. He had been able to touch a piece of vintage history and felt seen and appreciated in the process. My heart swelled. It was a silver lining in this upside-down crazy world to spend his 18th birthday with his old grandmother and family in Santa suits!

On the Fourth Day of "our Christmas RV Road Trip," my parents gave to me...

Reindeer antler headbands with blinking Christmas lights

Trying to make the most out of time with my elderly mom, I realized I needed some humor that night, so I brought out the blinking reindeer antlers. Yes, we even put them on the dogs. Laughter roared around the table as the kids took pictures on Snapchat with funny filters and ate our decadent desserts. My kids were now beginning to accept the divine craziness of their mother's holiday spirit. I believe they were actually starting to…. dare I say it… **have fun**!

It had been almost seven months since the last time we truly had fun as a family. It had been a perfect spring day of hiking at Icicle Ridge Mountain in Leavenworth, Washington, without a cloud in the sky, with the temperature hovering in the 70s and visibility that went on forever. My husband, daughter, and I decided to go for a spectacular mountain ridge view hike with 180-degree views of the valley below. What could go wrong? This was 2020, wasn't it?

I remember laughing with my family as we had just finished our trail snack of oranges and water. My husband told his jokes, and my daughter finally felt confident again and smiled. Time stood still in those moments as we admired the view together from a resting rock nestled high on the mountain.

My calves started aching in deep pain nearly halfway up the mountain, but I overrode my pain and pushed my body onward. At age 52, I didn't want to be considered the "out-of-shape mom" or be thought of as "old." I wanted to be a beacon of health by doing any physical thing I could imagine, especially since my passion was hiking in the mountains.

Then at 6000 ft, less than one switchback from the top of the mountain, I tripped over a root in the ground. I saw my left foot come forward with my ankle going in the other direction. There it was, the famous popping sounds of my tibia and fibula bones in my leg shattering, as I felt nothing left to connect my foot to my leg. Miraculously, my husband was there to catch my fall before I went over the side of the mountain.

On the 5th Day of "our Christmas RV Road Trip," my parents gave to me...

T-shirts from Big Sky Burger in Amarillo, Texas...

Texas felt like utter freedom as we crossed the state line. We were all ready to eat some good ole road trip burgers as everything seemed to be open here and not as "draconian" as we had been used to in the Pacific Northwest.

My mouth dropped wide open, and my heart was liberated as I saw that masks were "lightly" worn and then pulled down when ordering or talking—ha! People could sit unmasked in restaurants with groups of their friends, just talking and laughing, just like in 2019! I felt so free. Life really could be different; it could be full of grace, mercy, and faith

Oh, grace, mercy, and faith, I had gotten to know those three virtues well that year. God had continued to provide for my every need with my hiking accident. I was blessed with a doctor and radiologist who had been hiking directly behind us with a satellite phone. They were able to examine my leg, administer first aid by wrapping my ankle, and shared that it looked like a tri-molecular break while calling 911.

It took less than 90 minutes before the first team of three search and rescue paramedics arrived. They were able to administer first aid and pain medicine.

According to state law, there had to be five search and rescue workers to carry a stretcher. We had to remain there until additional heroic volunteers arrived almost three hours later to carry me down the 6,000 ft, 3-mile trail where the ambulance was waiting. It was as if I had my own search and rescue army of seven, in addition to my family and all the bottle-necked hikers coming down with me.

Once in the emergency room, the paramedic handed me off to Dr. Rose Gentles. Yes, that's right, Dr. Rose Gentles! God had even hand-picked this ER doctor for me, who treated me with grace and incredible mercy. She was the best ER doctor I have ever known.

Due to Covid, no one else was allowed in my room. I sat there alone, longing to have someone to endure this with me. Unable to truly process everything that happened, I reached out first to my "Sisterhood." They were a collection of six local prayer warrior women who had been dedicated to lifting up each other, our families, our communities, and our world in prayer for over twelve years.

I received instantaneous responses of loving words of faith, encouragement, and hope. I instantly felt their love and God's healing presence surrounding me as my heel was set into place, x-rays taken, and decisions about my next healing options. I knew I was not going through this alone.

Surgery was recommended immediately as soon as I returned to Seattle. Since this was pandemic times, I had to be prepared to go to a critical care hospital in the heart of Seattle. I was assured they would see and operate on me immediately. My heart sank. I needed God's help more than ever. I knew I had to supersize my faith.

On the 6th Day of "our Christmas RV Road Trip," my parents gave to me...

A really, really ugly Christmas sweater...

Spending time with our dear friends in Oklahoma and their beautiful ten-acre ranch was exactly what we needed. It was clearly time for the ugly Christmas sweaters to be handed out. I was thrilled to be in so much holiday bling, which was silly, joyful, and kept us laughing until we cried.

My daughter even persuaded our host to trade his *Game of Thrones* ugly Christmas sweater for her too-ugly-for-words sweater with a giant cat, glasses, and random sparkles. Who knew a *Game of Thrones* sweater could bring healing, belonging, and inclusion to a sixteen-year-old girl?

At dinner, the other restaurant guests gave us wide smiles and laughed as they complimented us on the sweaters in the almost canceled celebratory holiday season. If my being silly was bringing joy to others right now, then *bring it on*. I was now a warrior for intrepid compassion, and it felt great!

This year, I had been blessed with acts of fearless compassion by others. In a time of national isolation, a small group of friends chose to step up and support my family physically and emotionally by bringing family meals and the gift of encouragement into my home. When things get tough, you know how much you are loved by those who show up to support you, even when you have nothing left to give.

On the 7th Day of "our Christmas RV Road Trip," my parents gave to me…

A husky and llama stuffed animals…

The adorable husky and llama stuffed toys were actually Christmas dog toys from Petco. Too irresistible to pass up, I thought they would be great silly gifts for the kids. However, as soon as I presented the kids with these adorable gifts, our dog, without being prompted, jumped up and grabbed them out of my son's hands and started chewing on them. (I guess I should never forget my four-legged children!) We laughed until our sides hurt! Oh, how I loved that dog. She had a presence to make an entrance worthy of True *Grit* swagger.

I recalled the first day we got her. It was the day of my surgery on my leg and ankle. The surgeon successfully attached a six-inch rod to my fibula with a dozen screws, including two additional pins through my ankle to hold it all together, which he assured me we could take out in September with a second surgery.

Oh good, something to look forward to… NOT, I thought to myself.

After nearly two-and-a-half hours of surgery, I was ready to be taken home. I wish someone would have reminded me that I would be emotional after the anesthesia. I later read that when your body goes under anesthesia, you become unconscious, and since your body is being cut open (even for good reason), it is still considered a trauma. The body can not consciously react. Those emotions of the surgery will have to be dealt with at some point.

As my husband picked me up from the recovery room, he was ready to go. I felt extra lightheaded and wanted extra moments to regain myself. The nurse went over my at-home care requirements. I could tell the care directions were overwhelming him, so I talked in detail with the discharge nurse about all the procedures.

My emotions were all over the place. He felt I was disrespecting him by not letting him handle the nurse. I felt he was not honoring me compassionately. Couldn't he just be kind, loving, and supportive in the way I needed him to be now? Couldn't he just dote on me a little right now? This was not the place I wanted to have an argument as we let our frustrations with each other vent right there in the recovery room. It became the bitch vs. the jerk in front of everyone, and no one was the winner. Oh, how I wish I could redo that whole conversation!

As I arrived home, I had expectations of fresh sheets on the bed, fresh spring flowers in my room, and maybe even a cheerful card or verse on the bed. Clearly, none of that happened. My depressed teenagers met me at the door. They had nothing left to give me emotionally. I became furious with them for not showing that they cared by making things beautiful and loving. I cried as I felt my physical, mental, and emotional brokenness. I just could not handle any of it anymore.

As my husband walked out to clear his head and get perspective on the whole surgery conversation, a stray

Shepard puppy followed him home. Her love was palpable and immediate. We named her Ruckus, which emotionally got us through the summer.

Ruckus was a gift of healing from God in the form of a puppy who just wanted to be loved. She stayed in my son's room most of the time. I began to see him smile and break out of his shell. It was a miracle. Though my family could not take care of each other's emotional needs, we could take care of Ruckus, and she had enough love, joy, and puppy kisses for us all.

On the 8th Day of "our Christmas RV Road Trip," my parents gave to me…

CASH…(Our RV broke down and had to improvise quickly)

Say it isn't so! Twenty miles outside of Oklahoma City, our RV transmission went out. Of course, there was only one place nearby to fix it, and of course, they had to order parts, AND of course, the parts would not get there until after Christmas. NEW PLAN. *Okay, God, I can't wait to see how you make this turn out!* But God knew. We were able to stay with our friends, safe, sheltered, and provided with more laughter.

The beautiful Christmas Star was shining brightly in the sky. It was the Jupiter-Saturn conjunction that lasted for the next few days at sunset. It was a feast for the astronomer's eye and the dreamer's heart.

I wrestled so much with God this year. The surgery had unleashed my "dark night of the soul." It started with me waking up in the middle of the night during the June full moon. I just couldn't take it anymore. It was the feelings of deepest despair, a rawness in my heart that I could not hide, the rock bottom of feeling so *unloved* which caused a well of tears that overtook me like a giant emotional waterfall. Any expectation that my family would or wanted to take care of me was gone. I *felt* they were just not interested nor had the bandwidth to do so.

When my husband came out to check on me, he asked me what I wanted him to do. Did I need a counselor?

I wanted to feel his love for me. I wanted him to come and hold me and tell me everything was going to be alright. He did not.

I needed to tap into more divine love and surrender to God in a deeper way than I had ever done before, so I could make it through the night. I could not do this healing on my own. God was going to have to heal me from the inside out. I was broken—physically, mentally, and emotionally. I surrendered to God in the deepest lamentation of my heart to help, love, and show me how to get through all this pain.

The rocking chair I was sitting in was now moving to the rhythm of my breath. There was a stillness around me that was pure and vast. A deep peace welled up through me to fill my deep broken places and mend my wounded heart. There was nothing left for me to do except receive this divine gift of healing, peace, and trust in the healing process.

I felt that God was with me vibrantly now. I was going to make it through this hell and heal, find hope, and hold His unconditional love at my core. There was no turning back now. Every step was about healing, loving with integrity and faithfulness, and always choosing the zest of life over fear.

Throughout the next twelve months, I would wake up repeating the phrase, "I choose life. I choose life." I chose a life that was not hidden or silent but a life full of love, creativity, laughter, beauty, adventure, friendship, and abundance. A life in alignment with who I truly was.

I spent a great deal of time praying and meditating that summer as my broken body slowly healed. I found that I was starved for touch. Each night I laid next to my husband, having him caress my body. This felt more important to me than oxygen as I lingered as close to him as possible.

Blessed friends continued to stop by and sit with me. Little did they know how much I needed their encouraging words and to see their smiling faces. My isolation was slowly easing, and God's faithfulness to my healing was showing.

The doctor allowed me to slowly start increasing the weight I could put on my leg. Painful and exhausting at times, I started to get my strength back. I looked forward to returning to work and focusing on the opening of our elementary school.

Then, not to be outdone by mother nature, the unimaginable happened. The news reported that on August 27th, Hurricane Laura, a category four storm, would make landfall on the southwest Louisiana shore. The State of Louisiana and surrounding areas were in a state of emergency. Hurricane Laura rained down complete devastation, with at least 47 dead and over

$1 billion given in FEMA assistance. Did it have to be named "Laura"?

On the 9th Day of "our Christmas RV Trip," my parents gave to me...

Some target practice at an Oklahoma ranch...

Since it was Sunday, we decided to stay another full day and regroup, repack, and reorganize for our new plan. We had to leave some things behind with our friends since they just did not fit in the minivan. My husband was stressed and beginning to feel pressured to get to South Carolina before Christmas. We all were able to do a little target practice on their property for a change of pace.

The 2020-2021 school year in Washington state brought its own new set of obstacles. I was getting to be an expert on regrouping and reorganizing. When our governor enacted the official pandemic lockdowns in March, the school I worked at went immediately to remote learning on Zoom. Along with the rest of the world, we were all doing the best we could with the available resources to continue educating our students.

By August, however, I was dedicated to getting our elementary students back into in-person classes for as much time as possible. Compromise became the rule of the day, and no one got what they *really* wanted.

We ended up being one of the few Washington state elementary schools open for in-person/hybrid learning in September 2020. As a private school, we had the leeway to adapt in real-time to the fluid conditions of the pandemic, though we were understaffed and under-resourced, which forced us to always think outside of the box for creative solutions to our obstacles.

Our staff was amazing in their compromising resilience as they worked tirelessly to ensure the start of the school year was a success. It was a school year that I was the proudest to be a Co-Director. Depleted mentally and emotionally, each obstacle challenged me, and I grew in my faith and leaned on the grace of God in all things.

As our new normal in education commenced, my new roles included "temperature checker," "Covid attestation collector," and "mask up lady." These roles allowed me to keep the school open in person, connect with kids and families, and make the best out of a bad situation. It was the smiles in the eyes of the children that kept me going. I could hear their laughs and sometimes even their daydreaming and singing. Their innocence gave me hope for the future. A hope that was getting harder and harder to recognize by the late fall of 2020.

On the 10th Day of "our Christmas RV Trip," my parents gave to me...

Waffle House and lots of Starbucks coffee...

We were on the road again as we exchanged our 35 ft RV for a Chrysler minivan. We were overflowing with four adults, two large dogs, my daughter's luggage for a permanent move to South Carolina, and our Christmas gifts. I kept praying that the Christmas Star would guide us safely without drama as we all took turns driving 16 hours straight to South Carolina. Our only stops were at gas stations where we walked the dogs, Waffle Houses (which now had gluten-free waffles), and Starbucks throughout Arkansas, Tennessee, Mississippi, Alabama, and Georgia. Eating out in restaurants seemed like pure heaven after being locked down on the West Coast, so on the "10th Day of Our Christmas RV Trip," I topped off my day with whipped cream on every waffle and latte as a treat.

This year I learned to soak up every moment with a little extra bedazzle with those I truly loved. I recalled the late September day when my phone rang. It was Charlotte calling, and I quickly answered.

Charlotte had been my refuge in the storm of life. She was my safe spot and best friend since I first came to Seattle in 1997. She had been fighting off a terminal disease for the last five years, but the time had now come to surrender. It was the call I had dreaded, the final goodbye.

"Laura, I just want you to listen because I don't have much strength left in me now. I love you and want you to know how much your friendship has meant to me over the years. I love you. I have to go now. I love you, Laura." She hung up the phone. My heart sank. I wept deeply. It was a loss that crushed my soul.

I collapsed emotionally in early October. I took a week off from work to sleep, cry and heal. I found myself on the floor of the bathroom, emotionally broken. Everything started to weigh down on my shoulders: Charlotte's death and missing her funeral, the ever-changing mandates, the masks, the isolation, my daughter's move to South Carolina, the second surgery, the pain of deep physical therapy training, the suicide of our neighbor, the complete loss of friends near and far, the deep political divide that was making the country unrecognizable. It was all too much.

As I lay on my bed that week, wondering how to move forward in my life, all I could do was pray. With each prayer, an emotional and mental release happened until I could physically rest. I realized then the only thing that I could do now was sleep and heal. God was doing a deep internal restoration, so I had to mentally let go and trust in the new beginnings without attachments. God's got this, I told myself!

Sleeping for days to regain my physical, emotional and mental strength, I started to reclaim a zest for life. What wonderful synchronicity was coming next?

Well, God never disappointed me as I was led toward natural healing and naturopathic medicine. I took a wild herb remedies class that autumn and learned more about energic medicines and modalities. I focused on increasing my immune system with a naturopathic doctor who worked with me regularly on holistic healing for my physical, mental, and emotional traumas. I was introduced to additional innovative therapies, including biofeedback, mindfulness exercises, restorative yoga, and herbal supplements and teas. The results were amazing.

As I learned to walk again physically, I attended monthly sound baths to release repressed trauma in my body through vibrational resonance. I had physical therapy three times a week and a healing massage once weekly. My left leg was so weak that I barely recognized it. My hips were overcompensating and throwing my gate off. It was not going to be a quick fix.

Spiritually, I was adapting to life without my daughter. On her sweet 16th birthday, my husband could fly out and be with her as I joined through FaceTime video. She was beginning to smile again. She had become so strong and resolute over the last couple of months. Though I had cried regularly with the pain of letting her go, I could feel God was doing something amazing in her life. It was all happening without my help or input. Yes, the more I surrendered to His will, the more the healing miracles were happening.

My 23-year marriage was reconstructed from the inside out for the better. The hole which our daughter left in our daily lives weighed heavily on us both. We had to be strong for each other or be consumed with grief. Honest communication and intrepid compassion were needed for each of us in new ways. "All things work together for good for those that love the Lord" was my go-to verse, which I embraced on this healing journey. God was not finished with me yet.

On the 11th Day of "our Christmas RV Trip," my parents gave to me…

Chocolate Christmas Candy Extravaganza…

As we pulled into the South Carolina driveway late on the 11th Day of Christmas, we were met with extended family and a joy that only a beloved grandma could bring. We celebrated with our favorite chocolate candies and homemade cakes as we told stories and hugged the family we hadn't seen in too long.

Exhausting but worth it. We were all together again—cousins, uncles, and grandma—and love was overflowing everywhere.

During 2020, my family had become the small group of women that formed my "Sisterhood." We decided to meet weekly to get through this mess of a year, whether on Zoom or outside on the lake six feet apart. They were my rock of emotional support. And I could not have asked for a better "family" anywhere.

I became unapologetic in asking for prayer. I asked for and gave others abundant prayer like never before. We carried each other's burdens like a warrior carried his wounded brother from the front line. We saw each other through.

I met with others at the school for one-on-one prayer time. Mighty women of faith were standing up and being seen even in the height of pandemic lockdowns. In what felt like the darkest of times, I found women all around me sharing their light through prayer.

On the 12th Day of "our Christmas RV Road Trip," my parents gave to me...

A Christmas Eve Lights Adventure drive through small town South Carolina with Grandma.

WE MADE IT THROUGH! Our family got to Christmas 2020! We all survived. We indeed overcame each obstacle that tried to take us down. We laughed and cried along the way. It was a true adventure to be savored and one my children will never forget. I did not care if they thought I was silly, a little crazy, and weird. They knew they were loved, cherished, and a part of a family that always had their backs. It was my Christmas miracle—a wonderful, loving, upside-down, inside-out, nothing-went-as-planned Christmas!

Now, several years later, my family has found our road less traveled. A road we each had to forge ourselves with deep inner faith. We became each other's common denominator for love and acceptance when the world seemed cold, hard, and unforgiving. Grace fuels our lives and seeds our tomorrows.

Returning home to Seattle, me and my husband have held space for each other to grow, grieve and adapt individually which has made our marriage stronger. We have recently celebrated our 26th Wedding Anniversary with a fresh commitment of "all in" to cultivating the path to a life we both want hand-in-hand, step-by-step, never taking each other for granted.

We doubled down on supporting my son Jack emotionally through the last months of his Senior year in 2021, doing whatever it took to encourage him through the ups and downs. Graduation Day kept me in tears as story after story of the amazing tenacity of these young men and women was shared. The Class of 2021 were my heroes! They each faced incredible obstacles and pitfalls, but they showed up and kept moving forward, knowing their future was not clear; they trusted and had faith in each other and their dreams. God planted something truly sacred deep in their hearts for such as season as this.

Jack continued to transform through more challenging times, including a week-long white water rafting down the Smith River in Montana. Tragically, he mourned the devastating deaths of 3 friends, one who took his own life and two others who were Marines stationed in Afghanistan.

I have never seen him cry so much. He seemed to become a man overnight. Now, it was his turn to make his own way into the future he wanted to create. We watched as he confidently began a career in Aeronautical Mechanics and left the traditional university system behind. A rock of faith was born.

Living the sweet life continues as we set out for our next adventure. Remembering, with each end comes a beginning. God knows what He is doing so trust and let go, then leap into the future that waiting for you. Laugh with those you cherish daily, and never take for granted the power of the words "I love you."

Laura Ann Garris

Laura Ann Garris is a true-life adventurer who has been passionate about travel since her first trip abroad at 13 years old to visit *The Lady of Guadeloupe* and the pyramids of Teotihuacan in Mexico. Her avid curiosity and love of culture have allowed her to live in the Swedish Arctic Circle, lead mission trips to Haiti, and explore the best of Western Europe, including skiing the French Alps.

Already an international best-selling author of *Written In Her Own Words: Wise Woman Wisdom,* international speaker, and successful Life Coach, Laura Ann has appeared as a beloved guest on e360TV with *Your Time To Shine International Interview Series* and Holy Spirit Broad Casting Network Show of *Hope Follows* with Julie Kenzler.

Working as the Life Refresh Coach, Laura Ann inspires women to reflect on who they are and what unique gifts they bring to the world. Her intuitive wisdom, energy management skills, and Heroic Coaching practices teach women the dance between grit and grace for their own transformation into empowerment.

Originally from Atlanta, Georgia, Laura Ann now lives in Seattle, Washington, with her family and German Shepherds. Hiking through the deep forests of the Cascade and Olympic Mountains and exploring the pristine waterfalls and beaches of the Pacific Northwest are where you will most often find her, her family RV, and her next great adventure.

You can find out more about Laura Ann at www.LifeRefreshCoach.com.

It's Never Too Late To Be The Person You Were Meant To Be

By Susan Z Franklin

Bruce Lipton, a scientist and spiritualist who wrote the book "The Biology of Belief," and "The Honeymoon Effect," says in the first seven years of life, we are being programmed and that 95% of the results in our life come from that programming of the subconscious. When I took his seminar, he spoke of how when two people meet, they are on their best behavior. They come to one another as conscious beings wanting to lift each other up. Once the honeymoon is over, they let out those belief systems on each other that they hypnotically embodied from their first seven years. If they got a lot of negative programming, they are like two young children fighting each other's parents or whoever influenced them in those early years. This can be in romantic or family relationships. The Greek philosopher Aristotle said, "Give me a child until he is seven, and I will show you the man." This philosophy is nothing new, but Bruce Lipton has brought it to another level of understanding. To rise above this has been a lifelong goal for me that resembled a roller coaster ride.

My choices have often been interfered with, like an anchor keeping a boat tethered. This chapter is my testament to letting the anchor go. That anchor is my lemon becoming lemonade.

Here are some glimpses into my first seven years:

My first memory was of being in a crib at around two or three years old. *I asked myself why people were shouting and fighting.* I believe that most babies have this experience, which is forgotten as adults. Perhaps my memory of it helped me feel visible.

My mother told me often that I was conceived when she found out her mother was dying of colon cancer; her mother died at 48 when I was two. She said she couldn't enjoy me. I believe that I took from this that if someone is dying, my birth is irrelevant. I also feared that if anyone else died, it would be horrible and traumatic, and everyone would be fighting and yelling. I lived in fear of conflict of any kind throughout my life, yet it seemed to follow me everywhere. From this, I gather that what you fear becomes your focus, and you help in creating it.

We lived with my grandfather and my mother's brother after my grandmother died. I remember my mother saying my grandfather gave up living after her mother died, except when he was with me. That felt good. I don't remember much about my uncle. I just know that I felt and saw dysfunctional and fearful things, and my uncle was strange. He had many bouts with mental illness and was hospitalized for it, just like his mother was.

It also didn't help that my mother would cry to my father that she would die like her mother at 48 of colon cancer. It seemed like I was surrounded by my mother's fears, anger, distrustfulness, and bizarre behaviors that were not what you would normally expect. I wanted Ozzie and Harriet to be my parents or any other sitcom that portrayed nurturing mothers and fathers taking great care of the family. Even seeing the cartoon Bambi was scary since she lost her mother.

My grandmother, who passed away, came here from Poland with her sister. They left behind the rest of their family, who all perished in Auschwitz in the Holocaust. This is what I was born into. Little innocent me had a lot to deal with. I have compassion for how difficult it was for me to be a functional being. Yet looking back, there were people around me that were nurturing to me. No matter what I did or said, my father was always someone I could say whatever I felt. My grandparents, too, nurtured me, even when I didn't treat them right. Since my mother said my grandmother was a witch, I always looked for signs. My Aunt Florence was also very nurturing to me. Yet my biggest goal in life was to protect my mother so she wouldn't die, as she said, and to do whatever it took to make my mother happy. My fear of her dying held more weight than wanting anything for myself. Sad but true!

Yet, in reality, by not allowing myself to cut the cords with my mother way before now, I kept myself in a dysfunctional style of being for long past the expiration date of being a child in a dysfunctional home. Then in all my other relationships, I waited till they would betray me, as I felt in my family. I understand now my uncle and mother were suffering from their past; being an empath, I took on their feelings as my own. I suffered as much as they did; I was just a child.

I remember once being with a group of people that had been physically abused. In my case, it was emotional. I noticed that they knew that being hit was wrong, and you could see the scars, and everyone would be sympathetic to their plight. Emotional scars seem to be overlooked in our society, and if you even act like you have been victimized, it is your fault. That attitude of society helped me think I was the fault for everything, so I believed it was my destiny to fix them so that I could be okay. Now I see that in a higher sense of looking at this, it is understanding that you have choices and can walk away. Whether you stay or leave, the scars need to be dealt with, but staying in the same situation that put those scars there, with only you taking responsibility for them being there, is not conducive to being the best version of yourself.

My biggest obstacles were not feeling like I could speak well and not caring about being glamorous like my mother and sister. I suppose, looking back, that is why my grandmother kept saying to my sister and me, "stop looking in the mirror and speak up." I didn't look in the mirror as much as my mother and sister, but I also did not speak up.

In writing all of this, I see that I had no boundaries, which was a problem that I brought to every relationship I was in. I only seemed to have boundaries when I felt totally safe that the person wouldn't abandon me, which I was never quite sure they were safe either. In reality, I was taught to abandon myself in those first seven years, and I complied and did it throughout my life. It was not without putting up a good fight, though. I was resilient. I never gave up trying, but I too easily retreated when the whispers of defeat spelled trouble.

My mother wanted me to be popular and try out for the drill team in school. I left behind my dorky friends with whom I had things in common and did hang out with the popular kids for a day or two, but that didn't work for me. I figured my mother knew better than me what was right for me. She seemed so sure, and I wasn't. The drill team didn't work for me, either. I did instead what worked for me. *I went into the bathroom stall every day at lunchtime, wrote stories, poetry, and read books.*

The person I felt I was and my mother's desires for me were not in harmony. That made me feel like I was failing her. This relationship that I had with my mother seemed to replicate itself with other people as well. I would come to them with who I was, but they seemed sure of what they wanted and needed, so I would acquiesce to their desires and forget what mine were. Empathic, codependent, both, or just traumatized?

Being a great communicator was not my best suit. One of the obstacles was that I had a lisp until I was 16. I became shy and withdrawn after the fourth grade, and I was petrified my mother would die. In later years, I remembered traumatic events involving my mother, uncle, and doctors, where my voice would not express the shock I felt inside. Again, where were my boundaries? They were non-existent. My father didn't have any; I suppose I also learned not to. He was like an inflatable punching bag. All you had to do is punch him emotionally or figuratively, and he'd come right back up. I once asked my father, "Why didn't you protect me?" He answered, "I'm sorry I was too busy protecting myself." At least he said he was sorry. If I expressed any issues with anyone else in the family, denial or amnesia seemed to set in quickly. I suppose

I reconciled with myself that it was better just to forget it ever happened.

Writing was always an easier outlet for me than speaking. Since most communication involves speaking, it was difficult for me to overcome the sensitivity of everything outside of me. The safest place was inside of me. To exacerbate the panic I already possessed, my aunt Sally died when I was 7, my grandfather died when I was 9, and my aunt Florence died when I was 12. Not to mention the millions of children that lost their families and lives in the Holocaust, which were my ancestors. Their only crime was that they were Jewish. It was overwhelming for the sensitive, codependent, empathic being that I was. As I got older, I overcame my lisp and severe eating disorders. In the outside world, I did learn to speak well. I had my issues at jobs with other people, but it seemed to work out for me in the long run.

I lived with my grandmother and grandfather for a few months when I was younger and not getting along with my mother. My grandfather was so delightful and would tell me all these great stories, and my grandmother would cook meals for me and do my laundry. That felt good. When she said it was time for me to move, I immediately found a place to live. We had a few laughs about how I wouldn't eat her cookies when I was younger because witches poison little children. I was fully honest with her, and she was with me.

My grandfather helped me move, and I was happy to have my own place. I had a job at UCLA as a ward clerk with children that were autistic and other issues. I would ride my bike five miles through traffic. I loved the job. I got to see all kinds of things about children and speak to the parents and the children. I would also get to listen in on the doctor's rounds. Instead of being an introvert, I became a social butterfly. Having that job made me want to become a Special Education teacher. Instead, I married, worked in law firms, and wouldn't become a teacher until I was 50. Better late than never.

I remember getting very ill. I could barely breathe. I called my mother and said, "Mom, can you come here?" She said," You can come here if you want, but I can't come there." I knew I couldn't drive. Honestly, I believe I had pneumonia. I remember hearing gurgling sounds in my lungs. I probably was at death's door, but I survived. There was a store across the street, and luckily, they brought me groceries.

My future husband lived in the same apartment complex. Before we had our first date, I flooded his apartment. I was getting ready to wash dishes, but no water came out. I left the faucet on, thinking I could wash the dishes when it came back on. I got a call and had to go out. While out, I got a call from the landlord. He said that the water from the faucet leaked all over my apartment and the apartment down below. That was none other than Gary's apartment. Even though I had flooded his apartment, we still ended up going out and eventually getting married.

Despite all the red flags throughout my life, I continued to be extensions of my mother and uncle whenever I was around them. They were narcissists, and I was an empath. Not a great combination. Yet I still have to realize that I still remained hooked while ignoring all the signals that pointed me in a better direction.

My husband's mother, Sadie, was like a mother to me. She and I spoke every day. She had difficulties with her daughters, and I had issues with my mother, and we had the best and deepest conversations. She was my substitute mother, and I was her substitute daughter. It was a great match. When I had chicken pox, she took care of me and developed shingles. I felt so bad for her. but was grateful for how she took care of me.

I couldn't wait to have a child of my own. However, I couldn't seem to get pregnant. This was very disappointing. I finally did get pregnant, but I had a miscarriage. Then I got pregnant again and lost that one too. I gave up all hope of ever having a baby and was very sad about that. However, God said, "you will have a baby, don't worry. It will happen." That gave me some encouragement, but doubt still remained. One night I knew from the moment of conception that I was pregnant. The next day I told my husband I am pregnant. He asked when did this happen? I said last night. A week later, I took a supermarket test which said I was, and a month later, the doctor confirmed it.

Sadie loved my children as if they were her own. She even left each of them $30,000 after her death. My mother responded to Sadie's gift: "Why do you keep bringing the kids here? Do you think I am going to leave them money?" I said, "But Mom, they are your grandchildren." I didn't want to speak to her after that, but my father said, "Please, Susan, we are getting older; can you forgive her?" In truth, I was bringing them there because I knew my father would be dying soon. He was nearing 80, and I wanted my children to get to know my father before he passed.

Throughout my life, letting go brought me miracles. Yet I tended to hang on for dear life to situations that weren't a good fit. Why did I do this? Your guess is as good as mine. However, now in moving forward, the choice is not to be this way anymore. It is imperative and my intent. If I don't choose to do this, I will continue to have needless suffering that isn't even originally mine, and I will compromise my ability to be fully present. I know too much now to walk away from this realization.

I have repeatedly witnessed the person I was meant to be, and now it is time to embrace her. I'm writing about my past, but once this chapter is complete, I'd like never to speak of the traumas of the past. Time to leave it behind. Can I do it? Why not? You might say because I never did before. That is true. Whoever said, "You can't teach an old dog new tricks," was mistaken. I learn something new every day, and my curiosity and imagination remain intact.

The more I release my family of origin from my focus, the better I become. I'm sleeping great, my voice is getting stronger, and I am healthy. I can hike seven miles and not get out of breath.

These common characteristics all contribute to family happiness and strength.

Commitment: They make their relationships a high priority.

Appreciation: They let family members know daily they are appreciated.

Communication: They talk to each other about big and small issues.

How many families practice this? What a great world we would have if all children on this planet had families like this. Not to mention, it would be great for all humanity.

After my father died, my mother went insane and fought with everyone. Sure enough, she turned against my children. She wouldn't put them in a collage my sister-in-law created that had all the other family members. I was so angry. Yet silly me, I just continued months later as if nothing had happened. They say ignorance is bliss, but ignorance is not an excuse, leading to more trauma, not perpetual bliss. I was in a trauma bond relationship with my uncle and mother for most of my life. Many people saw what I didn't see, including my children.

What are the signs of a trauma bond?

Signs & Symptoms of Trauma Bonding

An abuse victim covers up or makes excuses to others for an abuser's behavior.

An abuse victim lies to friends or family about the abuse.

A victim doesn't feel comfortable with or able to leave the abusive situation.

An abuse victim thinks the abuse is their fault.

A trauma bond is a toxic relationship that is forged out of pain, abuse, and codependency. It's often a romantic relationship, but it can also be a relationship with a parent, sibling, or even a friend. *Resnick, Ariane, (2022)*

https://www.verywellmind.com/trauma-bonding-5207136

I often felt like my uncle was cutting me in half with a psychic sword. Looking at it through a different lens, by changing my verbiage, I can alter my perception. Instead of feeling like I was cut in half psychically, I am going to say this led to me having a protective sovereign sword inside of me that gives me the strength and empowerment to be my best self and live a life of being able to thrive no matter what is outside of me. Inside of me, that innocent little girl who was brought into a world of pain and sorrow is now the me I always knew I was but couldn't find. Now, I have found her. I intend never to lose her again.

My brother died suddenly on January 1st, 2019. It was sad, but his funeral was a loving experience unlike any other family event like funerals, weddings, or parties. My uncle tried to cause problems, but my sister-in-law's mother stopped the chaos he was trying to bring. Of course, his favorite subject, "money," was the catalyst for his intrusion. Though my mother and daughter were estranged, I rubbed my mother's back while I held my daughter's hand as my brother's casket was put in the ground. The funeral remained a tribute to my brother, and the chaos that my uncle was trying to cause would not materialize.

A year later, my mother was understandably depressed. My uncle said she was getting old. I remember walking through the casino, and he said,

"Look how she is walking and can fall at any moment and break a hip." He was so negative about everything that had to do with her. He had an agenda. I should have known since eight years before he asked me for money and said he would leave me all of his money, and when I said no, he said, "you will be sorry, and I'm very disappointed in you." I did keep my distance from him after that, but I never confronted him. I had replayed this many times in my life with my mother and uncle, where their behaviors or words were like daggers thrown at me. Still, instead of speaking up and letting them know how much they hurt me, I cried and felt the pain, but when it was gone, I went back for more as if nothing had happened.

I now make the choice to let go of my feelings of anger and revenge that still reside in me. It doesn't serve me. I choose now to release it. This is imperative for my salvation. There is no other choice now for me. Let me share with you what occurred before I released it completely.

To sum it up quite simply, I spoke the truth after my uncle was horrible to my sister and mother, then turned it on me. Quite a common story with my family of origin. He disowned me and said he would disown my sister, too, if she didn't call me a liar. I didn't lie. It was all the truth. Not my truth, but the truth. I dared to speak the truth.

Looking at this, I realize it is time to forgive myself for not knowing any better.

Besides the beautiful gift of having two daughters and two granddaughters, my greatest accomplishment after they were grown was becoming a teacher. I met Barry in October of 2008. Being a teacher fulfilled my purpose, and meeting Barry was a great experience. For the first time in my life, money was not an issue. He showered me with love, attention, and abundance. My confidence grew like never before with no obstacles. We had found each other, and both of our lives were enhanced. We found in each other everything we always desired in a mate.

I believe my uncle lost control over me once Barry came into the picture. He seemed to want it back. I remembered he said before the altercation, "We should all be like Susan." I also remember my sister saying, "Susan, you always know the right words to say." My mother and I seemed to be getting along quite well, and I felt that the loss of her son was enough, so I forgave her. However, my uncle's actions brought everything to the surface for me, and once I felt all these feelings, I had to address them and see them for what they really were. You learn the most from challenges rather than what makes you comfortable.

I no longer suffer from insomnia after my incident with my family of origin, and my voice is getting stronger again. No depression exists in me anymore. I am happy and have gratitude for all the beautiful things in my life and the lessons that brought me here.

I learned that when confronted with bad behavior from others, either speak up at the moment with words of wisdom, then let it go. Why harm yourself more just because someone wanted to harm you? Why continue the job that they began?

Second, if people aren't a good fit, even if they are family, keep your distance or leave. Why put yourself through that just because of the label that they are your family? There are many wonderful people out there who feel way more like what a family is meant to be.

To help me with communication, I did Toastmasters beginning three years ago, and my speaking improved significantly. The other thing that helped was doing Lumosity when I broke my ankle. The brain games helped me slow my brain down, and then my speaking improved substantially. I excelled at all the games that measured speed, memory, attention, flexibility, and problem-solving. After doing them repeatedly, I got into the highest categories in all sections.   Another triumph is I no longer have eating disorders. After more than 40 years, I am so in touch with my body that when I eat sweets, I feel full and need to stop. I have become a normal eater. I've read that 97% of people never get rid of their eating disorders. I did.

The author of this book Michelle Faust recently invited me to a seminar called Speak Your Truth. I saw myself in a way that I never did before. I wasn't afraid to Speak My Truth. The continued support is music to my ears.

Being in this seminar allowed me to see that I was much more than I ever thought I was. I was amazed at how motivated and excited I was to spread my wings. I had lost hope that I would ever feel this good again. Now I was going beyond where I had ever been before. My insecurities have revealed themselves, and I'm ready to leave them behind. They are my past and don't belong in my present. I now have fellow travelers on the road to being their best selves and creating what they have to bring to the world. We are all there for one another.

The lessons that I have learned are invaluable, and I am grateful for it all. I don't regret anything. An example of how I am altering my way of looking at things every day is on Facebook. I was getting some negative messages. I unfriended the negative messages; all I was left with were positive ones. Such as :

The secret of change is to focus all of your energy, not on fighting the old, but on building the new. ~ Socrates.

An emotionally healthy partner doesn't try to change you; they hold space for you to be who you truly are.

Always value your peace more than people's opinions. ~ Thoughts Wonder

Every day I look at Facebook and see these great posts. People think of Facebook as being negative, but you have to get rid of the weeds to have a beautiful garden.

That is a great example of what I am doing in my life now. By releasing the weeds from my heart and soul, I am open to new people and experiences.

When I was a teacher, my classroom was where I was able to give 100% to every child and their extended families, and I know that I was able to change lives for the better. My methods were not traditional, but they worked. As a teacher, I love simplifying the information rather than complicating it and hoping they get it. I was like an energized bunny, jumping all over the classroom. It worked. My students' standardized test scores rivaled schools where the children had all the advantages in life. My school was Title One, which meant children from disadvantaged backgrounds. We were a team, a family, and we all worked together to have everyone succeed.

Looking back at who I was, I was always a bit of a quiet rebel. I thought of myself as so compliant and people-pleasing. I went along with the plan, but I was always plotting how to go beyond. Finally, my wish to become the person I always yearned to be has arrived. I've found her, and I never want to lose her again. She is a combination of many things. Sometimes she is an introvert, and sometimes an extrovert. She is my authentic self.

Whatever energy you choose to focus your thoughts on is exactly what you attract into your reality, according to an NLP concept.

I will monitor what I focus on, ensuring it is what I want.

Now it is time for me to live my life daily with love, light, and purpose. I no longer choose to judge myself by others' words or actions, but the most important person I would like to impress is me.

Spiritually I was born Jewish, but I feel more aligned with seeing how all religions are connected rather than a means of separation.

I believe that every religion has as its base: "treat others how you would want to be treated." If people aspired to this, religions would unite rather than separate, in my opinion. I have friends from all political camps, beliefs, and nationalities who are all one and the same.

My paternal grandparents studied Christian Science. My father and grandparents taught me that the mind is strong and can heal anything. In later years, I listened to Science of Mind on the radio on my hour-long drive to work every day for over ten years. It resonated with me and still does.

I had wanted to be an author since I was seven years old when my Aunt Sally died. My grandparents saw her soul go to heaven and told me about it. I can still see them in the corner of our yard, and it was very peaceful to hear this. The next day I went to school and wrote a story that amazed my teacher. At that moment, I knew my destiny was to be an author. Yet I have yet to be published. I realize that writing is more than just a hobby. It is what I love to do and how I express myself best.

Now I will be published in two books soon for sure. This book, of course, and another book called "The Art of Connection" destined to be an international bestseller. I have nearly finished my trilogy, "Telepathic Odyssey, From Echo to Planet Earth." I wrote a play with my students called Peaceful World for Children, and they performed it. The play was the precursor to my trilogy.

When I retired, I just kept writing. My editor said she wanted it to be 200 words rather than 300 words. I looked through and took out references to my life; what was left was a dystopian and utopian fiction novel. I continue to write, and now I have a trilogy.

I believe that speaking my truth has now become imperative. I realize that being authentic and assertive are the keys to having great relationships with yourself and others. The truth does set you free. I have the awareness, and now I also have the courage.

One of the most important tools to keep me present is to remain conscious and mindful in each moment. I've been doing this now for months, and it is becoming a habitual way of being. Now it is proving to have longevity. This eliminates reactivity and is being replaced with being able to make wiser choices in each moment. Acceptance is another key attribute rather than giving in to the disappointment of unmet expectations.

Who am I now? I am a sovereign, intuitive truth-teller, wife, mother, grandmother, teacher, and aspiring author. I speak, write, and teach from my heart.

My life is mine, to make a choice to move forward and leave the past behind. I declare it is never too late to become the person you were meant to be.

Susan Z Franklin

Susan became a teacher in her 50's. Teaching has been a heartwarming experience where she was able to achieve great results with children in poverty and second language learners. When she retired, her desire was to take what she accomplished in her classroom and extend that out into the world on a broader basis.

In addition to being published in two books this year, she is also working on educational endeavors with her former principal and great friend, and she is almost finished with a trilogy called Telepathic Odyssey from Planet Echo to Earth that began as a play she wrote with her third-grade students they then performed.

Susan knows the importance of educating children and giving them the tools necessary to be the best versions of themselves as the way to have a better society where humanity can thrive. Her desire to do her part in working towards this and collaborating with others is the direction she is moving in.

She is a credentialed Teacher, with a B.A. in Psychology, and an M.A. in Education with an emphasis on ESL.

She resides in Phoenix, AZ, with her husband, Barry Franklin, and has two daughters and twin granddaughters.

susanzfranklin@gmail.com.
602-350-5097

The Pleasure and Pain of a Wonderful Life

By Diana Grasso Barrett

Three Youthful Goals

I see the world a bit differently, with more clarity and less innocence. Thirty years of marriage, motherhood, and divorce have changed me forever. I am stronger, wiser, and more courageous than ever before. I am the Tin Man, the Scarecrow, the Lion, and a little bit of Dorothy. The girl who lit up the room, the girl who loved life and spoke to the world through her bedroom window, and the servant child of Jesus who continues to have faith, for he is the reason for all seasons; the good, the bad, and the ugly. Through it all, we need to find gratitude and grace.

I had three goals as a young woman. I always wanted to have a business, get married, have a beautiful wedding, and raise a family. I was married in my late 20s, and as a young couple, we had common goals. They were pretty standard, the goal to complete your bachelor's degree before marriage, the goal of opening a savings account, budgeting together for the wedding, and eventually start a family. My personal goal was to start a small real estate business. We were worker bees; I was the salesperson of the two at the time, taking all sorts of sales classes at the office and in Chicago. He was learning by the lead of his father and a partner. Two excellent examples of business knowledge as we started our lives together.

Much of my work ethic I learned from my mom and dad. My first job was as a cashier at my father's small grocery store at 16. You build integrity when you work. You also have structure at a young age. First, you go to school and work part-time. Next, you go to college, work part-time, and then work 40 hours a week! Your body and mind are trained to get up at the same time every day so you can work for a living. I learned this very young and continue to believe in this value system today.

My parents did not have the opportunity to go to college. My dad thought he was in line for the family grocery business in Chicago. His dream was shattered when he discovered my grandfather had sold the store without informing him. So my dad had to find new ideas to support a growing family. My dad and uncle analyzed an offer to buy a McDonald's franchise; after all, we lived near the first one in Des Plaines, Illinois. At that time, they wanted $3500.00 each, and my uncle thought it was too much. The deal didn't happen, so my dad searched for a grocery store he could buy.. He partnered with a friend; it was small, with five aisles. The lines were short, constant, and neighborhood friendly. The butcher counter was in the back, lined up with homemade Italian submarine sandwiches we made from scratch, all in rows on top of the cooler. Back then, employees in the neighborhood had 20-30 minute lunches and would grab and go. They were a big seller, and our customers were regulars. I still enjoy packaging my own groceries to help out the cashiers when I shop to this day.

When I was in my mid 20's balancing college, love, and life in general, I worked part-time for Century 21 and fell in love with listing and selling people's homes. As values were rising steadily. I tried to budget every penny, but my fiance was not interested. I was lucky to get him to give me $500.00 each month to deposit into our wedding account. It was a struggle. I was paying my school loan debt, monthly auto bill, car insurance, and saving for our future. I taught aerobics part-time nights and weekends at Bally Health and Richard Simmons clubs; we worked out together often, it was a thing. Do you remember the one-piece tights in shiny colors and the sweater leggings with little bikini bottoms? Yep, that was me. Let's not forget the headband and full curls.

Like every American, we wanted to own a home. So we bought a condo before the wedding with our savings of $10,000.00. It was a condominium in a golf course community. I knew it was a great location, so we wrote an offer. It was a perfect two-bedroom with cathedral ceilings on the second floor and a fireplace. It was spacious, with one large master bedroom and one TV room. It was affordable and in a good location. We planned for children, but for this young couple, it was too early, for a few reasons, to start thinking of parenting, and I decided to wait.

I felt great, I loved life, and I was beaming! I was young, stunning, and a size 7! I had my mother's genes and looked very much like her when she was 21. This was the time of Flashdance, Thriller, Footloose, and the movie Ghost; it was the 80's! We sold the condo after two years; after five years of marriage, we welcomed the arrival of our firstborn son. We made some solid improvements to our first home, which gave us the equity to buy the home of our dreams.

I loved working on my homes from the very beginning. I had been watching my dad repair and care for our childhood home my whole life. He was hands-on, and I wanted to be as well. We were a blue-collar family raised with much pride. Watching my dad paint, wallpaper, and hammer away felt good. Dad was extremely handy and did all the work himself; there was no extra money to spend foolishly. He was a good man and a good husband to my mother, taking great care of our home and family. We had great respect for both parents. Even though they were both very strict, we felt tremendous love in our home.

After watching my dad all those years, I realized that I was learning from him, and he was my teacher. I was learning about the delicate care, detail, and love he displayed so we could enjoy a beautiful home. It was small, safe, and filled with love. He died suddenly, just weeks after we closed on our second home. I soon realized the lessons were there, and Dad was with me in spirit to lead the work our 30-year-old home needed. My hands show age from all the hard work, and I am proud. I am the hands-on property manager, including plumbing, but I will never take on electrical work. Nor did my dad. You have to know your boundaries.

By the age of 33, we owned our dream home. We were the youngest on the block. When I found this beautiful Tudor for our family, I was pregnant and about to deliver my second boy. I overheard the first offer on the table, and as the Realtor, I knew what I needed to do to get the deal. I needed to make my offer more desirable, so I kept the closing date blank. A good salesperson finds the pressure point of the seller, and I knew the president's wife for BP Amoco wanted her children to graduate from the local high school.

My husband didn't come to tour the house; he was too busy at the office. I knew it would sell fast, and I was right; it was a dual offer. The home was 3500 square feet, listed for $333,000.00. It was in a class-A neighborhood. You know what they say about location; I was spot on in my real estate decisions. I knew the hot markets, the more desirable areas. I had an eye for locations likely to grow and be in demand. I knew real estate would bring us significant equity for retirement someday. My husband saw my skill set; he fell in love with real estate because of my career and real estate knowledge, and soon after, we both wanted commercial property for cash flow.

My children were about 3 and 5, and we were unfamiliar with the commercial market. I thought that was for rich people. Looking back, I wish I had taken commercial classes because it is so lucrative. I wanted to be active in brokering the purchases, but it was easier and smarter for my husband to hire an experienced commercial real estate broker in his office building. That commercial real estate broker found us the deal that would change our lives and take care of us through retirement, FOREVER: for as long as we live and as long as our children live. We took a chance; it was a single cash flow investment property purchased during our marriage. Like many young people in business, we had no idea what we were doing, but the loan was approved because the new trucking business backed it financially.

We loved looking at homes and going to auctions. We bought homes that sat on the market, bought a few new construction properties and quickly sold them, and bought what we call buy-and-holds. At that time, we dressed up, and we were served champagne and

hors d'oeuvres. We were in love; it was grown-up fun while being young. I did the due diligence, and we had equity and profits five properties later. By the time I was 35, and he was 37, we had the family home of our dreams, one commercial cash-flowing property with 50 garages, two cell towers, a free-standing garage rental, several parking spaces for semis, and a vacation home to rent in sunny Arizona! We were part-time investors and didn't even know it. We were just having fun buying real estate. The business and the investment property took off. While my husband built the business, I managed the home corporation, the house, the kids, and my mother, who was ill. I did not have to go into the office any longer, and my active investing became passive as rent rolls came in.

I loved raising my children. I remember when mothers in the neighborhood said they could not wait for school to begin to ship their kids back to class after the holidays. "Who says that?" I thought. I loved having my kids home! I would not have traded it for anything. We had so much fun together. I loved being the gardener, the pruner, the decorator, the party planner, the chef, and the travel agent for the family. Sea World,

Budweiser, Legoland, Safariland; the Gorillas came up to the car door! Disney California, then Disney Florida! We traveled to Tahoe and the Virgin Islands and more. Even simple vacations to St Louis continue to make for laughable conversations today. The railroad trip! Yep, the trip that the boys will never let me forget! Lol. We also visited New York and Ellis Island; every visitor to this country should visit the 9/11 memorial!

We had so much fun spending time together and with the neighbor kids. Our neighborhood had many stay-at-home parents; our bunco group was 40 women! A few stay-at-home dads came by with champagne popsicles to share with the moms and mojitos during garage sales. We had group playdates, park district events, library reads at the river, picnics, and Brookfield Zoo visits to see Olga, the old walrus, and Boo at the ZOO for Halloween. We were always at the local pool when we could be, ordering pizza with neighbors for an easy night. We had a great neighborhood, and my boys had many young friends.

My favorite memories of my boys were the simple moments. My youngest was such a hugger and played with my long hair all the time; until I told him it probably was no longer appropriate as a high schooler. I also remember his older brother loving on him all the time! I have so many pictures of them smothering each other. We had little tables and little chairs and even little recliners! How could I miss these moments and go off to the office? I was fortunate and a very lucky lady to be able to stay home and raise my children. My kids were inseparable all the way up to my youngest's high school graduation, and they both went to a university together! My eldest was a transfer student from the local college, and my youngest was a freshman. How perfect, right? The moment we all wait for. The time to be an empty nester, more time for us!

God and Faith

At age 35, I knew it was time to learn more about the faith I was born into. I felt it was important for our children. I strongly believed in God but did not have a relationship with him. I had so many questions. So we eagerly found a Catholic church and a Lutheran church to shop for our growing family. Immediately, the Catholic church felt redundant. I went to a catholic grade school and walked to church every Sunday, a requirement of my Italian Catholic parents. Although I felt it was good for my childhood, my parents never joined us. My dad was always very sick and needed to rest on his day off to have enough energy to work for the family during the week. The grade school and the church were a block away. I have fond memories of all my teachers and grade school friends, and I keep in contact with them through Facebook today.

We decided on the Lutheran church because the pastor introduced himself to us, and a neighbor in the pew put her hand out to introduce herself to us as well. I hadn't felt so welcomed in a church, ever! I joined a women's Bible study, having no idea what the Fruits of the Spirit were. I liked our new church so much I began to volunteer on the communion team. I met so many women and men, but my husband had no desire to join any men's groups, nor was he interested in getting to know anyone at the church. We stayed there as members until my eldest was in 8th grade. At that time, we were told about a newer non-denominational church in town, so we thought of visiting. It was a square building called the Yellow Box. My kids loved it, and so did I, but dad was not feeling it.

There were many Sundays I went by myself to church. I continue to go every week and enjoy the message God has for me. Was this not a joint decision to raise our children in faith? Why did we baptize them? I continue to have these conversations with my children that go something like this. God only has 10 rules. They are on a tablet, pretty simple. This nation was built on faith, which is what our nation needs most, especially today.

Simple expectations from God include all good things. It's not tough to be good, and it's not tough to tell the truth unless you have something to hide. It's not hard to praise and be thankful; you only need to have gratitude in your heart. It's not hard to be kind to others. Your heart will sing when you see a stranger's joy or comfort from your help. If you reap and sew, He will reward your life.

I know so many people who know and love God: their lives and families lives have been blessed. They believe that after they work the field, so to speak, give their money freely to the church, and serve others daily, it is God who rewards their faith in him.

I've been serving strangers for years, going back to my 20s. I have always had a heart for the elderly, especially shut in's. As a young girl, I wanted to bring them food and sit with them for company. My little town must have had a program at church where the adults cooked, and I delivered. A Meals on Wheels type of operation. We will be there someday, and I would like to know that a stranger would like to sit with me. That's the power of Jesus Christ. God first, others second.

Life was full. Life was comfortable. The days came, and the years flew by in the blink of an eye. I thought I was an independent woman! What do you think? I thought I was on fire. Taking care of the home, taking care of my wheelchair-bound mother full time, getting a healthy dinner on the table as often as possible, working 60-70 hours a week, and checking in with my boys as they were now older, and I was less needed. I achieved my goals, raised my children, and were preparing them for college. I applied for two jobs, was hired for both, and regained respectable employment after 25 years. Hourly is all I could get with no proficient computer software experience. I loved my two new part-time jobs! The local school would train me, and I loved managing the local chocolate shop in town. The owner allowed me a flexible schedule, so my husband and I could travel. That's what we wanted. All he needed was a phone or an iPad. After all, my husband has been the boss now for 20 years. He didn't need to be in the office any longer; we had a wonderful manager with 20 years of experience with our company, who allowed us this freedom for years. I was a lucky woman, and he was a lucky man. We were at the finish line. The final quarter.

Some things in life are just not apparent. God has a plan for you; He is grooming you for the next season. That season could be a sunny summer day with Lemonade on ice, or it can be an ice-cold storm. In my life, it was a subliminal progression over the years. Then pow. I knew something wasn't right in my marriage, and what was going on came to the surface; it arrived quickly and suddenly, and all of my intuitions were correct. Looking back, I was too busy dealing with my family and work and ignored the red flags before me. It's easier to stay in the land of comfort. I ran the family corporation, and my office was our home. I ran it pretty darn smoothly for 30 years! But, when your questions fall on deaf ears with your partner, you must dig deeper for clarity and the truth.

I will not allow myself to be hurt by what I am not aware of, and I have no desire to know the secrets of my marriage any longer. People in our lives continue to come to me with new information; I just listen. They, too, now have the truth before them; it continues to rise to the surface, even years later. God calls on us to speak nothing but the truth, and he knows that not sharing in a marriage or partnership is a lie. That is between the liars and God. I had no time to worry about things beyond my control, things I cannot change. Ever heard of the Serenity prayer in AA?

The Lemons…Social Justice and Divorce Law

Divorce law is a civil court matter. Unfortunately, within that law, several areas lack the support of those that seek justice. Social Justice is one of those areas. The #MeToo movement continues its journey, bridging the gap between 1965 and today. There is so much more work still to do, but #WeToo is also in need of reform. We are women across the nation, on meet-up hikes, in coffee shops, at the baggage claim, my neighbor in an airplane, or my virtual associate in another state. The stories are the same. We are living paycheck to paycheck, driving for door dash or uber to make enough money to put food on the table for ourselves and our children. We are young moms and older stay-at-home moms, and we not only require a change in the area of Social Justice but in the area of Business Law.

While the defendants keep the business, get awarded more assets than the plaintiff, and clearly are awarded assets acquired during the marriage, worth over the IRS income line, the judges and attorneys continue to fail their clients and community. Those who are in contempt never see a jail cell, those who are publicly fined in court, are often charged minimal fees, and those who miss deadlines ordered by a judge are not penalized by loss of assets in the decree. How can we be mentally stable? We have lost our life as we know it. Some of us are misplaced, which is highly unusual; some of us are left without a home, and some have no health insurance, all life-changing.

I fought for my health insurance because who doesn't need insurance, right? We need it for our physical self and, more importantly, our future mental wellness. I was lucky, I had a support system of friends, a few community neighbors that made that call when needed, and a sister who insisted I live with her through breast cancer. What happens to those that are not as lucky, with no one?

I supported the system my whole life. I paid my taxes, I paid into social security, and by volunteering and contributing to my community, I made it a better place. The one time I needed the county and the state, the law wasn't written to support me, the stay-at-home mother for 30 years. No one speaks up because we are busy, daily, in survival mode, or living in fear. You, the system, failed my children too. We had a beautiful life. If you took care of me, I would not have lost all this time scrambling to start over. I would be a financially independent woman in my home and in my community and had been locally working as a Realtor for the past two years during the best real estate market in history! If options were available to me that no attorney or judge put before me, I would not be worrying about my future and if I will run out of money someday.

When life looks good, really good, and feels so great that you feel you need a pinch, young ladies, you most likely do! I guarantee it. Let this be my love letter to you. "Things Happen," says Suze Orman, a financial expert.

Where are you in your relationship or marriage? Are you complacent? Is your spouse or partner dismissive privately and in front of others? Are you being controlled in subliminal ways? Are you afraid to leave? Are you afraid to ask questions, and more importantly, do you get clear answers? If you are unsure of your place in your relationship, please check the CDC website or google IPV, Intimate Partner Violence. A new acronym. Violence is not just physical anymore. It can go under the radar for many years; it can be financial or psychological. If you see red flags, address them. If he or she shuts down your concerns, take note and plan ahead. You are your own advocate.

The CDC now recognizes this ongoing problem in our nation; they recognize it as an epidemic and advise that it can be preventable. They have developed a video on their website defining strategies for our health and others. They explain that we all need to work toward humility and bring humanity back and that divorce is a traumatic experience. More than ever, Christian men and women are on social platforms teaching people how to treat partners God's way. Divorce law is outdated, can and should be changed, and completely rewritten to protect all women and men in the area of business, business entities created during the marriage, and social justice.

The W2 spouse cannot hide his/her employee income, and the divorcing spouse usually receives alimony for life. Now is the time that the spouse who wants to own a business, therefore creating an entity or entities, if married, be required to disclose and acquire ALL marital party signatures at closing, including but not limited to real property, real estate, and business: to protect us all, ensuring transparency, which will lead to financial security for the mother of the children and the aged spouse close to retirement age. To split properly, what is assumed to be fair. Everyone assumes fair to be 50/50. What most people aren't aware of in divorce is that 50/50 means AFTER what is left and payable to all, including the attorneys. The deep pockets take and walk away with what they choose. The attorneys and the businessmen. It is still a man's world in divorce law.

This is God's season, and he is leading me to new pastures, new people, and new women as we form our new families. Relationships are so very important, especially when family is gone or you simply don't have family. I am the third youngest remaining of 50 family members, and that's my side! After divorce, you must build boundaries and rebuild your circle, and you need to surround yourself with those who will help you flourish. If you're my age, and I'm going to be 60 this year, it's your final quarter, and you most likely do not have 25 years left. Are your long-time friends and family there for you? Do they go out of their way for you at the drop of a hat? Do they check in on you? I am forever grateful to those that do, and you know who you are. When you have fallen to your knees and have been to dark places that you have never seen before, you get back up by faith, and when you stand on your own, you must have genuine people surrounding you.

It was a priority for me to keep in touch with everyone as my life changed before me. I ensured the texts and phone calls continued, even if my husband and the court displaced me out of state. I made sure to assure my closest cousins, nieces, and nephews on both sides, that we would all be ok in this new relationship and status. I thought that my ex-husband would divide our assets, share with me what was rightfully mine, and we would be this blended family like most that still hang out together. Boy, was I wrong. I didn't realize I became the enemy; my ex-husband put the line in the sand. I left my marriage, I didn't leave my family or community, but some left me, and the county told me I was to move out of my home, which I groomed for 30 years. I'm the same person who welcomed family and friends; I'm still here.

I have learned that family doesn't have to be blood any longer. Strangers will treat you better when you are trying to survive, and real friends will draw you closer. The darkest of times for me will always be when I discovered real depression and suicidal thoughts within the last two years. Those peaks and valleys I hope never to see again. I now know what a good majority of our nation deals with, and we as a society need to take time for people in our lives and on our soil. We are all too comfortable living out our days and not doing enough for mankind. I questioned my faith at least three times in three years; I fell to my knees twice and asked for his grace. Without support, you become a statistic. I'm so thankful for a counselor. His name is Michael, and he saved my life.

Here is my thank you to everyone else who checked in and stayed. Near and far, I will forever be grateful for the calls and texts from a few family members, a few neighbors, and a group of wonderful genuine friends! Watching the county give my home, where I raised my two boys, to my ex-husband, during COVID-19, when it was rightfully mine to keep, was devastating. I had no choice but to separate every item within 3500 square feet and 30 years of memories and home furnishings, all by myself, while going through breast cancer surgery, removal of my gallbladder and lymph nodes, and going through radiation during my 58th birthday. Wow, thank God for Sisters! She gave me a home so I did not have to spend the rest of my mother's inheritance on rent. She gave me a bed and a roof with love. You can't put a price on that. It will forever be in the books, the time in my life that made me the woman I am today. I do not take one moment for granted.

I picked myself up and dusted myself off for the last time. I'm working hard at employing a plan to achieve my goals. I get up at 6 am to grind and learn new things like any 25-year-old starting out. I'm learning the difference between financial fiduciaries and how financial advisors operate from bank to bank; and that they are all different. I am learning about ETFs, stock trades, annuities, 1031 exchanges, SDIRA's, I bonds, Treasury bonds, and real estate investing strategies. The latter takes most of my time, 60 hours a week without pay. I work out when I can, and that's not much right now. Walking seven to fifteen miles a few times a week does my mind good for now. I can't get up at 5 am to get it all in; I need that extra hour. If I am tired, it will not be a productive day! It needs to refuel!

I want my boys to see that I can and will thrive again before I leave this life, as I did for many years before I married. I was young, beautiful, vibrant, and popular among my friends. I had everything going for a young girl. I had many close friends, male and female, and we had a great childhood outside of Chicago. I didn't have a perfect life, but I was always happy. I was always smiling, never crying, and never sad. My whole life, that just wasn't me. I know that that's what drew my husband to me when I walked into our Personnel Management class for the first time in college.

My kids know there isn't anything else more important to me on this planet than them. Not money, not a house, not a car, not anything. If I were thirty, I would have had 30 more years to find a partner and enjoy love again, and I could successfully meet my personal and financial goals. If I were 40, I would have 20 years to succeed; if I were 50, I would have 10. I am 60. I'll do as much as possible with the window I have, and with God's grace, I can live comfortably, find true love, buy things I need and want, and enjoy life, and my boys, as life was meant to be.

Lemonade

Every day, I grind the lemon halves on a manual grinder. I have several paper cuts on both hands from all the networking, classes, webinars, podcasts, and specialized knowledge from the previous 12 months. Although I am in the process of separating the grind, the lemon seeds, and the skins, I am pouring purified water into the pitcher with the proper amount of less sugar, please. It's going to be tasty! I rise and grind every day, it is hard and time-consuming, but it will be so worth it. I am overcoming obstacles and seeking solutions to overcome adversities, and my trunk(my spine) becomes taller and stronger every day. My roots are spreading deeply, and I am creating a new foundation.

Who doesn't like homemade fresh squeezed Lemonade on a hot Chicago summer along Lake Michigan? I look forward to the first glass and will certainly post a picture of me sitting on the lake in enjoyment, and I will gladly post on the Lemonade Stand Community Facebook page! It will be a moment in time when I am in a good place, emotionally and financially, celebrating the calmness of my favorite city on the planet!

How is your foundation? If you feel this story resonates with you, or someone that is in need of help: or you are a retired Attorney, or someone in a position of power willing to assist in a Landmark case that changes divorce law in Illinois and nationally, you can find me at Diana Grasso Barrett on Facebook.

#WeToo wants your feedback and assistance to change people's lives.

Diana Grasso Barrett

Diana Marie was born in Park Ridge, Illinois and raised nearby in Norridge, a small blue-collar community just one hour outside of Chicago. She has nothing but wonderful memories of her childhood and her high school experience as a cheerleader and homecoming queen. The families were mostly Italian Catholic, and the core values of the neighborhood was built on faith.

While completing her bachelor's degree at Elmhurst college, she was a full time Buyer for Panasonic Television purchasing globally and domestically, completing her education for a Real Estate License in Illinois, and planning a wedding all at the same time. Her lifetime work consists of positions that include realtor, retail, sales, geriatric activity director, fitness Instructor, and event manager. While raising two young boys in Naperville, Illinois she was also a full-time caregiver to her mother who was confined to a wheelchair. In her lifetime, her love for real estate has allowed her to own single-family homes, condos, townhouses, patio homes, rentals, auction properties, warehousing, and multi-purpose land, Diana is concentrating on what has always been her passion, real estate investing.

When she is not working, she is enjoying her time with her havanese shih tzu Snickers, another family member. She enjoys finding the next new huge park for Snickers. She also loves to hike in Arizona and Illinois and discovering the West coast. Her bucket list includes a trip to Italy, visits to Montana and Utah, and a long love for a used black corvette!

If you find any of her story resonates with you, or you know someone that can help make a difference, or you would like to be part of the change into the future, you can find Diana on her private Facebook page @Diana Grasso-Barrett, as she continues to develop her business page and social media.

coffeeandmartinis@gmail.com

Chasing Hope

By Julie Kenzler

My sister Tammy and I agreed to share our morning devotions the day after a cheery conversation on the phone. She shared hers first, not because she was the oldest of us siblings or her time zone was three hours ahead of mine, but because Tammy was passionate about sharing Bible insight that was encouraging in practical ways. As soon as I saw her email IN HER USUAL ALL CAPS WAY, I read it and then shared mine. That was our last phone conversation and email exchange before tragedy struck.

On a crisp fall Sunday, Tammy was feeling heartbroken about the recent loss of her sweet dog Peanut of seventeen years. Getting on her motorcycle to drive into town and read her Bible at her classic Starbucks was Tam's way of escaping the pain of being home without Peanut. Tammy never arrived at the coffee shop. Without even a warning, she was struck by a car that crossed the center line on a rural Indiana road. The man, the driver, was returning home after being at two bars that day. Yes, he was under the influence by double the amount of legal BAC (blood alcohol content).

Honestly, though I have tremendous hope to share what came after this horrible loss, I hate talking about the entire crash. I hate it so much. So, please allow me a moment of space for a few seconds. I often take a moment to pause and reflect on the special people in my life and what they mean to me. I hope this is a key takeaway for you because you never know when a loved one will leave your life.

It's wise to know when we need to press the pause and reset button. Retelling this story is gut-wrenching. But let's do this together and chat as I recall how that tragic, horrific day consumed our family's lives for the years to follow. The consequences and aftermath were more of a steamroller that wouldn't stop, all from one person's choice to drink excessive alcohol, get into a car, turn the key, and drive. A steamroller: a heavy, slow-moving vehicle with a roller used to flatten the surfaces of roads during construction. Get this second definition: an oppressive and relentless power or force. That was what our family was suddenly thrust with; a life running from a steamroller.

A Sister Is Forever

I hold closely in my heart all our endearing memories growing up, like a gift wrapped with a beautiful red bow. Our family lived in northwest Indiana near our extended family, who were a big part of our lives. Childhood to teenage years was filled with adventures and memories of ALL KINDS.

Summer beach days at the Dunes National Park, traditional holidays at Grandpa and Grandma's house, scary movie rentals from the local video store, thrilling rope swings, and pedal boat rides on our lake were some of the times we shared that filled our memory tank. But then there were the crazy times, like when Tammy was driving past the speed limit in our neighborhood to spend the day at the beach when a community security officer began chasing us. Once you left that gated area, they legally cannot chase you down. In Tammy fashion of hilarious moments, she laughed hysterically as she raced past the gate. YES! We did it! And our beach crew couldn't come back until later in the day after that officer was off duty.

Oh, the places we explored! A visit to Tammy at her university was never without bushels of laughter combined with plenty of energy expended physically. One year at Easter, my parents, brother, and I spent the weekend with Tam, and she took me spelunking in a cave. I can vividly feel the cold air in that dark hole as I reminisce about the experiences she would plan for our "sister time." We were covered head to toe with mud! Our parents' faces were shocked as they saw us enter through the hotel room door. Let me tell you, this was way before the *Tough Mudder 5K* events were even a thought. Have you ever made an egg for breakfast in the entire peel of an orange wrapped in aluminum foil? Cooked over a campfire? It's so delicious, and I doubted Tammy when she was preparing it. But, after an afternoon of canoeing to the island where we were the only people there, you don't argue about the menu. Tammy taught me to try new things, foods, and experiences.

As with all sibling relationships, you endure more than happy, jolly times. There are seasons of pain and hardship. Our biggest one came when our dad died of a sudden heart attack at the young age of 46; I was 16 and Tammy 22, with our other siblings aged 6 and 20. Lament, grief, sorrow, sadness, and disbelief are a few of our many tumultuous emotions. In the years that followed, my siblings and I traversed different paths with our lives, learning to live without Dad in our unique stages of life.

My path of life found me in sunny Arizona, graduating from college and marrying a great guy from my home state! Crazy how God puts people into each other's paths. We both were from Indiana but met in Arizona, and both our dads had died at young ages, and believe it or not, their names were both Jack.

People say that when one person is taken, another one is gained in your life. I only realized this when Grandma died. "Aunt Sis," as her many sisters and family members lovingly called her, was a gentle and strong woman of great Christian faith. At her funeral, I mentioned to my sisters how sick I felt. A few weeks later, I found out I was pregnant. My first child would be special because he or she would be named Jack if a boy or Jacqueline if a girl, after our father's name.

As I journeyed along my pregnancy, Tammy and I began to talk more on the phone. Then, the day she met my first baby, her first nephew Jack, she was instantly in love. Soon after, my siblings and I made a deliberate effort to stay connected. Funny how things happen like that, and you don't worry about all the lost time. You just pick up where you are and embrace new times and memories together.

Relationship reunions and meaningful moments bring out the art in people, whether through music, writing, or on canvas. In her gifted way with words, Tammy wrote this significant poem to summarize our family's own reunion and reconnection. The unique flower in the poem represents my firstborn, Jack, the first of the next generation in our family.

Poem By Tammy Hale
Different paths we take
Thru the flower patch of life
The starting point is the same
At the rose garden we begin
Thorns are sharp, fragrance is sweet
Vibrant colors surround us
Hand in hand we embark
We drop our hands as we each take
Different paths. Different interests.
Where are you?
Memories, dulled as we look for our way.
Separated by circumstances
So many beautiful flowers.
Suddenly our paths rejoin
At the bloom of a unique flower
We bend low to view this flower
We look up at each other
Smile.
We are together again.
What a wonderful place to reunite.

This was the beginning of a new era of adventures for Tammy and me. She frequently visited us and quickly became my children's favorite business trip babysitter. Whether it was her visits to our town or our trips to hers, Tammy put her best spunky effort into playing with the children, cooking delicious meals, arranging scavenger hunts, and leading treks to the desert trails or wooded forests.

Having a sister who is also your close friend naturally leads to the creation of the best memories. We were each other's confidante, encourager, and shoulder to lean on. I miss not seeing Tammy and hearing her voice. I miss her laugh. I miss her ALL CAPS writing in her emails. I miss the articles she would send me when I struggled with parenting or other life issues. I miss not being able to hear her struggles and remind her what a great person she was. I miss that she was fully engaged in her time with you, showing that you matter so much to her; no phones allowed was Tammy's motto.

Making the deliberate effort over the years to fill our hearts and photo books with memories was an important tradition. Our trip to SeaWorld in California was a favorite memory that tops the charts. The most hilarious thing happened when we arrived at our reservation for "Dinner with Shamu," Tammy bought tickets for SeaWorld Orlando instead of where we were in San Diego! We laughed till we cried, nearly peeing our pants! Finally, after running back and forth to customer service, we conquered the challenge and sat poolside with Shamu, enjoying a splendid meal.

Our last time together was over a weekend when she visited me in Arizona in January of 2013. We enjoyed our usual routine of lying by the pool, hiking, getting Starbucks, playing our favorite game, Boggle, and attending the children's activities and sports events. It was the first time we had been together on the date of our dad's death, which was in 1985. We had a special time together, and we were already planning out our visit for the next summer. My oldest son, Jack, was entering his senior year in high school, and Aunt Tammy wanted us to visit her for a special mom and son, aunt and nephew trip. We never took the trip, and this saying haunts me, "If you fail to plan, then you plan to fail." But then, the summer got away from us, and we didn't visit. I still feel sad for not seeing her that summer, for not making it a priority, and for not planning that special visit with my oldest son, who had been about to go off to college and enter adulthood.

Why do we live with regrets? Losing my sister taught me to fuel my regrets into living a "Carpe Omni" life to seize it all. In fact, author Daniel H. Pink suggests we use our regrets of the past as a guide for better living. The emotions caused by regret—sadness, and disappointment—can be all-consuming. Through his research and study, Pink insists that the healthier and better way to handle regret is by maximizing them to live a fuller life that flourishes.

May you recall something of regret *only* to sculpt it and change it into a learning experience, a purpose, or a banner of what to live for.

The Phone Call and Aftermath

November of 2013 was a mix of tears and knots in my stomach. Receiving the dreadful call from my sister Tracey could not be compared to anything I can describe. I became numb hearing her words about the crash. Tammy was gone. Saying the word "died" is still very hard for me. Saying she was "killed" hurts excruciatingly. But that is what happened. A man who worked far from his home was in town spending time at two bars that Sunday morning instead of devoting those hours to his wife and child. I'll never understand.

The aftermath and devastation that followed one man's choice to drink excessively and get behind the wheel of a car caused deep roots of pain for the years to follow.

The court case was held one year later. It was grueling and horrific for our family. Watching this meaningless pain and grief consume Tom, Tammy's husband, was more than one could bear. But all of us, family and friends, did our best to emotionally keep Tom on a healthy path.

Jury decision: not guilty. Reason: the jury did not believe beyond reasonable doubt that the offender's blood was transported correctly to the lab. Can you imagine a hurricane or maybe a tsunami in the courtroom? How this small town allowed it to come to this point was a nightmare to us all. The fact remains: that man did drink double the legal limit and drove a car instead of getting a ride. He took my sister away from us. Anger. Despair. Hopelessness. Where would our family go from there?

Nearly two and a half years after losing Tammy, her husband stopped trying to move forward. Loss. Trial failure. Suicide. Her husband took his life with a gun. Numb feelings once again. His heart was so broken after the tragic loss of his wife. Our family was constantly worried about Tom's emotional state. But, really, God? Why? We were making progress toward helping Tom to create a new life for himself. We could have helped Tom. I wanted to believe that. Once again, grief hit our family like a bulldozer flattening a dilapidated house.

So much extended tragedy from one man's wrong and selfish choice. He could have called someone for a ride. Everything inside me just boils when recalling those awful days. Something good must be made out of all of this. Something. Anything. God, why did that man have to hit my beautiful sister?! I recall many screaming and crying fits for those first two to three years.

The Painful Grief Work

Days were spent feeling hatred toward that man who took my sister. My next feeling was that maybe Tammy wouldn't want that man with a daughter to be locked away from his family. I knew forgiveness needed to happen one day when I was ready. But, first, I needed to go to the ER for my heart, emotionally.

That visit looked more like a two-year graduate program. I spent two twelve-week sessions in a support group called Grief Share. I learned so much about grief and coping strategies. I learned that you are never alone with grief. There are people all around, ready to support you and hold you when you feel faint and weary. The people in my support groups played a critical role in my life back then. They got me. They understood me.

I found a grief counselor I grew to depend on for professional counseling. Our two years together were such a process of transformation. She taught me so much about myself and coping with losing Tammy. The best part about our time together was prayer time.

Dawn, my counselor, spoke the most beautiful prayers over me. It was a life support system.

The journey of grief work didn't stop there. I needed to do whatever it took to face this unwanted guest named "grief." My personal and unique way of dealing with grief was facing it head-on. Time was spent reading stacks of grief books, hiking in the desert mountains to feel a sense of openness, listening to worship music, and talking with God so much that He probably needed a break. Actually, I don't believe that. He is too big not to handle our problems, small and large.

Music was healing for me. I would sit on my family room floor listening to words that gave me hope and encouragement. After dropping off my children at school, I would listen to worship music, sitting on the floor by my couch. As I sobbed those tears of overwhelming sadness, I set my head on the couch as if I were resting in Jesus's lap. It felt so real. He felt so real. I know that my strength and healing came from those moments.

Writing and journaling my grief and fears, hopes and regrets, along with feelings and experiences, became therapeutic to me. As part of an important step in the healing process, my heart and head did find a way to forgive. Am I still angry? Yes. Do I want to tell the offender all the pain that was caused? Yes. But what good would it do? God spoke so clearly to me about how He would use this devastating and tragic loss for good. Still, I couldn't imagine that ever happening.

Adding to the painful domino effect of one person's choice to drink and drive, while on this journey of looking for hope beyond losing my sister, there were moments my children wondered if their mom would be okay. Struggles crept up in my marriage due to neglect. My focal point was engulfed on a road called grief; my husband was lost and confused about what to do with his wife. What was happening to us?

A Hope Switch Turns On

The story doesn't stop there, friends. For you see, when you have HOPE in Jesus, and you work hard to understand and heal from painful experiences, joy will make its way back into your dim life. My family truly was such a light of sunshine for me. I recall tightly squeezing one of my son's hands in the car on our way home from swim practice. I was crying so deeply that I began to hyperventilate. You know, the kind of crying that takes your breath away. The crying spells would come on like a tidal wave so unexpectedly.

One day, I recall having unusual feelings of pure elation and joy. Feelings that were somewhat stifled deep down for a while. It was about two years after losing Tammy. I was telling my youngest son how much joy I felt inside. He said he also noticed I was the happiest he had seen me in a long time. I smiled a lot more. I wanted to be present with my family and in on anything fun they were doing. I had serious FOMO, fear of missing out. This may have gotten a little annoying for my teenagers, not wanting Mom to hang out with their friends while they watched a show. What troopers my children were to make a way for me even in their independent teen years.

Throughout my journal writings, I noticed a consistency in my stories. There was a blend of humor and practical relevance that could possibly bring encouragement and hope to others. One such story was when I wanted peace and quiet, packed my car with an exercise mat, and headed to a park. As I lay in the sun, I suddenly heard loud whirring noises. The landscapers had arrived for my party of one! It was hilarious trying to gather my things and flee. That moment I recall laughing so hard and telling Tammy about it. Wow, laughter is critical to our happiness and health.

I decided to put all the writings and experiences from my journal into a digital blog in April 2015, naming it *Julie's Blog for Hope*. It became more obvious how God's hand was in my grief recovery. He was there through it all and continues to walk by my side. He can do that for you, too.

When I was a mom of little children, I had this desire to write a book. From my experience as a newspaper reporter in 5th grade and high school, I must have thought I was destined to be an author. The decision to write a book began around the year 2000. I was a mom of three kids and, for sure, an expert enough to write a book. How fun would it be to write a book and give it to my children when they grew up? I came up with an outline, a title, and even a cover design. That was the end of my book-writing dream. I have no idea how moms of little ones write books!

During the 2020 pandemic, I revisited and rekindled that book dream. But, it turned out to be a book that wasn't what I originally intended. The blogs of *Julie's Blog for Hope* turned into a new blog website *Hope*

Follows. God made it clear to me that this was the book to write: *Hope Follows*, a book about real-life stories that bring encouragement and inspiration. We face hard things in life, and I found there can always be hope. HOPE FOLLOWS the hard stuff, and we need to reclaim the joy that is ours.

After a long journey of researching and learning how to write and publish a book, the box arrived in December 2020. I cried when I got it because that wasn't the book I was supposed to write. This was a book that came out of losing my sister to a tragic crash. The book publishing journey was an emotional one. But it's what God gave me to write, and I needed to follow what I was being asked to do. To spread hope through written words.

Guess what! My kids got their mom-written book for Christmas that year. This family effort was quite the project, but one that I am very proud of, and I am thankful for the support of my family and many dear friends. The feedback and responses were great. It was quite encouraging to hear the impact the blog and book were making.

Hope Follows Gets a Promotion

After being interviewed about my book on a television show for an international network, the producer was in tears and said he had not heard HOPE talked about as I did. It's not every day you get asked to have your own show, but I do love to talk. He invited me to host my own show. After much prayer and deliberation on fitting this into my busy schedule as a teacher and a mom of a senior in high school, it became very clear this was the direction to take.

Hope Follows got promoted from paper to air time. What a fun ride it's been, too. I have met so many people and shared their stories of hardship and struggle, loss and challenge, and the HOPE that FOLLOWED those trying times. As I reflect today, I would change it all to have Tammy back. I would give up the book and broadcasting opportunity to have Tammy back. I would rather have my sister here enjoying her family and friends and the love and service she devoted to people she didn't even know. I didn't need that type of book or the show. I could have written another book and not had a show.

Then, God gently stopped me and said patiently, "But, Julie, you do have Tammy. She is right there with you. In your heart, in memories, in your writing, and speaking. It's not a 'one or the other' option." I realized and finally accepted because Tammy had been taken so tragically, and I fell so hard in deep grief that when GOD BROUGHT ME OUT OF THE PIT, I was obligated to share my story. To teach and inspire others to find Hope.

I sit strangely at peace, knowing that while I wished Tammy had never been struck that horrible fall day, I have a heart and eyes that are opened up to see life from a new perspective. This refined focus on God's purpose in my life now has opened up numerous opportunities to share the heart of "Hope Follows."

I now interview people of all ages about their real-life struggles. We have had guests share their hard stories about miscarriage, depression, anxiety, suicide, chronic disease, military tragedies, marriage storms, divorce, addiction, homosexuality, rough seasons of parenthood, aging parents, life-threatening illness, and career setbacks, to name a few. BUT IT DOESN'T stop there! There is always HOPE. Each story shared on my show offers a most incredible and inspiring *HOPE FOLLOWS* story that came after their hard times. Can you relate? What is your hard story that hit you in the gut and took you down to your knees sobbing? Look closely now, and see the hope that came after. It may have been small or big, but you'll see it out there.

The title of this chapter is Chasing Hope because isn't that our human nature when hit with trauma and challenges? We cry tears for hope to come to us; we literally chase it down in our need to feel better. The truth is that when you believe, hope will follow.

May you open your eyes and heart to the possibilities God has for you. What dream do you have that has been crumpled up and tossed into the wastebasket? Hold on a minute! I see the crumpled paper! Go, look. It's there on the floor and never made it inside. Alright, take a deep breath and pick it up. Slowly uncrumple it and open it up. Aim for that dream because you have a story to tell.

Julie Kenzler

Julie is an avid writer and promoter of finding "HOPE" in all the hard things we face in life. Her writing passion began when she had her own newspaper column in the fifth grade; how that short curly haired, silver wired mouth girl always dreamed of writing a book one day. Her blog writing journey in 2014 led to her first published book in 2020, "Hope Follows". Within one year, Julie found herself behind a camera as an international broadcaster bringing people's hope-filled stories to 7 continents and 190 countries on the Holy Spirit Broadcasting Network. Platforms including Amazon Fire TV, LG, Facebook, Roku, YouTube, and more continue to explode with Julie's authentic and wise inspiration. She will have you laughing one minute and crying the next, only to leave you more ready to chase your own hope story.

Whether it is a room filled with a captive audience or on a stage, Julie's voice of experience and charm bring authority in teaching those around her to have confidence and boldness in exclaiming lost joy. She has spoken and taught on a variety of stages to include independent business owners, ministry leaders, and educational directors.

God has been her anchor and rock to walk through some very difficult and dark days. Her heart fills up to the brim anytime she spends with her husband and adult children, whether that is on bikes, Cornhole in the backyard, crazy brain games around a campfire, or running to be by their side when needed. Making memories and serving her family is on the top of her to-do list. She lives with the motto, "Carpe Omni." Seize it all. Don't hold back.

juliekenzler@gmail.com
https://www.hopefollows.com/

The Grace of Love

By Michelle Faust

In the darkness before dawn, I hear my husband, Dean, desperately calling for me, "I have to get to the toilet!" He quickly falls off our bed onto the floor with a boom. He is at my mercy as, at this point, he is wheelchair ridden and partially paralyzed.

As I drag him across the tiled floor, I pray for some adrenalin-powered super strength to help him—no such thing. Unfortunately, he immediately loses control of his bodily functions. A trail of feces accompanies us as we make our way to the bathroom. I see frustration, indignity, and disgust on his face as he rolls around in his own feces. And then it hit me—I don't have the strength to get him into the shower as he is essentially dead weight. No matter how much I love him, I can't endure this journey alone.

How We Got Here

Let me back up. Dean has suffered from chronic back pain for years but refused surgery in 1995 when a specialist recommended it. Twenty-seven years later, it is no longer possible to postpone surgery. If he does, he will be wheelchair-bound for the rest of his life. Dean's medical situation is complex. He needs at least two surgeries—one on his cervical spine and the other on his lower lumbar.

Dean's back injuries initially happened in a military parachute accident. Luckily, the Veterans Administration (VA) provided a whole battery of testing and agreed to pay 100% of the medical expenses related to his back injury.

Panama Bound

The desperate need for Dean's surgery and our decision to move from Arizona to live full-time in Panama coincided. It made sense to investigate the medical options in our soon-to-be adopted country. We have owned property in Costa Rica and Panama since 2005, with the dream of retiring in Central America. That time in our lives had arrived. One of the many reasons for choosing Panama to be our home is the excellence in medical care. We have looked closely into what's available here, which rivals anything in the States. Through additional research and a personal introduction, we connected with a neurosurgeon who impressed us from the very beginning.

We were fortunate to get a referral from a medical friend to Dr. Alejandro Sossa, on staff at The Panama Clinic in Panama City. Our relationship with this talented man began with international phone calls while we were still in Arizona. He speaks fluent English, as do most professional medical providers. We were able to expedite the process by sending recent MRIs, X Rays, and medical charts for Dr. Sossa's review. Also, Dr. Sossa did all the work to set up the approval with the VA to cover all the expenses directly. There is a Veterans Hospital here, but the Foreign Medical Plan with the VA allows veterans to choose their facility as long as prior approval is made.

While Dean's lower lumbar causes him the most pain, the surgeon insisted on repairing the cervical spine first

Michelle Faust

as it was so unstable that he feared Dean could come out of surgery a quadriplegic if this surgery wasn't performed first. To help with the lower back pain, Dr. Sossa gave Dean eight pre-op epidurals. One shot on each side of the spine, so sixteen shots altogether. We said, "Bless you, Dr. Sossa," as the pain relief was temporary but a gift for the first two months of recovery.

After several pre-ops, we scheduled the surgery for August 5. Dr. Sossa determined that the surgeon would have to enter from the anterior (front) and posterior (back) to fully rebuild his cervical spine. Dean pleaded with the doctor to do the entire surgery from both angles in one session. He didn't want a third surgery added to his treatment plan. Dean is a retired physician, so he fully understood the risks. Dr. Sossa agreed, pending Dean was stable and his vitals strong on the operating table.

The Panama Clinic is a state-of-the-art hospital barely three years old. Their location within a small mall has all the conveniences of a grocery store, pharmacy, department store, and several restaurants. The mall is also home to a Marriott Residence Inn, which is an ideal setup for family members of hospital patients.

The Surgery Saga

We arrived for surgical check-in at 10:00 am. Dean and I shared our thoughts and fears and held hands in prayer. He asked me to promise to uphold his wish to do both surgeries at once. Then, I kissed him long and hard before the hospital tech wheeled him away.

Communication breakdowns can happen if you are not fluent in Spanish, which I am not. The professional staff

139

speaks English, but nurses, techs, assistants, and receptionists generally speak only Spanish or, at best, broken English, about my skill with Espanol. I had the option to wait in the surgical waiting room, his pre-assigned hospital room, or have the flexibility to take a break when needed in my nearby hotel room. They required only my cell phone number to reach me. Great! I had a business call, and the hospital room would be perfect for that. I made the call and was lying down for a rest when I got a text from a mutual friend who works in the hospital. He said Dr. Sossa had been trying to reach me to let me know the surgery was delayed. I checked my phone for missed calls, but a blank screen was all I saw. It turns out someone had mixed up my phone number with Dean's. All the calls went to Dean's phone, which was turned off.

Even though the call was not urgent, I lost confidence in being contacted promptly if the medical team needed my presence. So I parked myself in the surgical waiting room and prepared for the endless wait. He eventually went into the operating room at 3:30 pm to be prepped and given anesthesiology for the surgery. At 12:30 am, Dr. Sossa opened the surgery center door and called me.

"We've finished the anterior surgery; he's doing fine but has been under anesthesiology for 8 hours. I need your permission to continue the posterior surgery." I responded, "Well, I don't like making the decision, but I promised Dean I would emphasize his desire to get both surgeries done tonight. Is he stable? Are vitals good?" He replied, "The medical team agrees that he is doing well." So, I gave the go-ahead and prayed I had done the right thing. Dr. Sossa sent me a text at 5:30 am, answering my prayers of the night. Dean was out of surgery and in the recovery room.

He was placed in ICU after 14 hours in the operating room. That's a lot of trauma for a body to go through. Fortunately, he passed the initial post-surgical exam of moving his limbs and wiggling his toes. I showed up at 9:00 am when visiting hours started. He was in some discomfort but in good spirits. The anesthesia had not quite worn off, and he had pain meds on board; it was like having a conversation with a funny drunk. Visitors were not allowed midday in ICU, so I left to do errands and get some rest.

At 6:00 pm, I was back in the room, and Dean wasted no time telling me, with a hint of worry in his eyes, that we might have a problem. He had lost function on his left side and no longer had command of moving his limbs, fingers, or toes. Dr. Sossa ordered an emergency MRI to confirm what he already suspected – a clot had formed at the incision site. Back in the OR, Dr. Sossa reopened the incision and found the clot; he pulled it out of Dean's spinal cord like a lifeless but deadly snake.

Back in ICU, Dean and the medical team began the long and painfully slow recovery process. Although he did not have a stroke, his symptoms were similar to one. We would have to retrain his brain to communicate with the muscles and nerves in his body. A baby in a man's body. Our new reality hit us like a Dodge Ball smack in the face when Dr. Sossa said in a quiet voice, almost a whisper, "I don't know if you will walk again, Dean." I began to think of this clot as the devil; his visit left Dean crippled, damaged and drained of his old life. Patiently, Dr. Sossa explained the details of the damage done by the clot, an evil whisper that crept in like a murderous strangler, squeezing out the lifeblood of his spinal cord. It would be days, even weeks, until we knew the extent of the damage, possibly months before any tangible recovery would be realized.

Like A Tragic Comedy

The total hospital stay (ICU and main floor) was 11 days. If it were a stage play, it would be a tragic comedy. Full of funny moments along with complex physical challenges. In the ICU, he tried to convince me there were people after us. He said he heard the patient next door "talking about us." He thought they were on a mission to swindle us out of money to bribe the immigration office so they could stay in Panama. He was one paranoid man. Pain medication can do strange things to a person.

The day after moving to the main floor, he was relocated to a room directly across from the nurses' station. Why? He was a bit of a bad boy, and they wanted to keep their eyes on him. The night nurse caught him climbing over the railing to get to the bathroom because he didn't want to pee in his pampers, and the nurses left the urinal out of reach. Even with his antics, I always witnessed the staff laughing with him. The nurses were probably both sad and relieved to see Dean discharged.

Dean was understandably a bit demonstrative about getting out. A hospital room is no place to heal. He was released in the evening hours, wheeled to my hotel room, settled into bed, and the medical assistant said, "Goodnight, someone will return to get him for physical therapy in the morning." They were then out the door. Gone. I was on my own. I wondered how in the world I could care for this man as I am not a physically strong woman.

And that very first night was when he fell out of bed desperately trying to get to the toilet. I had decided to sleep on the couch even though we had a king-sized bed. I just wanted to give him his space to sleep well. Right before dawn was when I heard a fearful, urgent-sounding moaning from the bed, and it wasn't from the side I had tucked him in. The room was too dark to see, so I followed the sound. "Dean, what's wrong?" I heard him calling to me, then realized he was trying to crawl to the floor towards the bathroom. I started this chapter with that story because I wanted to share how difficult life can become in an instant and what emotions erupt in the process.

I had pure hatred for the blood clot, whose post-surgery presence changed our lives drastically. I screamed at this devil in my rage, "You have the power to kill, but Dean is stronger than you. You can't render his mindset and tenacity to survive and improve. He'll beat you. He will @%$#&*) beat you, mother...... From the moment you left his body, he has gotten stronger every day. As much as I curse you, I praise God even more. As a bee dies after doing its damage, so do you. You no longer have the strength to kill or injure. We will beat you by the grace of God and the medical team and the village of friends who surround us with love and care."

It Takes a Village

After that rant, I cleaned Dean up with washcloths and towels as best I could. The hotel maid earned a big tip this day. I calmly called my friend and neighbor, KC, letting her know I didn't think I could do this alone. Like an angel from heaven, she and another neighbor, Chuck, took the bus to the city, arriving at our hotel room late afternoon. KC said with a smile and a positive attitude, "Come on, let's get stinky in the shower, then you clean up, and we'll go downstairs and get something to eat." KC and Chuck together had the muscle power to get Dean into the shower on the shower seat and scrub him clean.

Refreshed and with renewed hope, the four of us went to the restaurant (Dean in his wheelchair) and let the doting staff take care of us. It's comical how Dean handled his glass and fork during that first outing. He had tremors and limited function, so food and beverage would fly randomly onto one of us and then onto the floor. The staff was gracious and patient with him, as were our friends.

We needed to stay three more days at the hotel to access physical therapy twice a day. It was a drop in the bucket of what he would need, but it was a good start in building strength before we headed home.

Although I appreciated the proximity of the hospital and the food and maid service provided by the hotel, I knew we would thrive more at home. We had a village there waiting for us to return, willing to step in and help in any way they could. Some took on cooking for us, taking Dean to the gym while we awaited home PT, Jonathan was his shower giver and beard trimmer, and plenty of others were there to share a glass of wine, an off-color joke, and simple friendship.

We had a chair that doubled as a toilet and shower seat, portable urinals everywhere, diapers, cleansing wipes, bandages, spit buckets, and pills organized in AM and PM doses. I played many new roles but adapted because of my unconditional love for Dean. I learned how to dress and get him to the toilet, brush his teeth, and teach him to feed himself. I was the retriever of everything he needed and a provider of love and reassurance. Our mode of transportation started as a wheelchair, graduated to a walker, and finally to a cane; it was a triumph to get to the cane.

About a week after arriving back in our condo, I made an appointment with the nail senorita who does at-home manicures and pedicures. I find it humorous that I DON'T DO TOES, but somehow I could endure the accidental spraying of urine and clean up Dean's feces. I asked the nail senorita to take care of Dean's nails first. He is routinely meticulous about grooming his nails, but they were overdue. I've told Dean many times that he should enjoy a pedicure sans polish. He has consistently refused to dabble in such a feminine ritual. I could be the boss now and insist he gets his nails done!

None of his improved mobility would have happened so quickly if not for Anthony, a young Panamanian physical therapist provided to us at home by the VA. He is a quiet and dedicated man to his profession and his family. While working to strengthen muscles, they each enriched their minds by practicing their second languages. They shared stories and learned from each other about culture, history, and how each, in their way, was self-taught in learning about life and survival. Anthony is and always will be a dear friend. The bond stretches far beyond the medical connection.

Taking on the Role of Caregiver

The heart and soul of this story is about relationships, my love story with Dean, our relationships with others like Anthony, and my own growth and understanding of who I am and what I am made of.

I confess I am, at the very core, a selfish person. This may come from seeing my mother care for others first and never caring for herself. She never dared to dream and died a bitter person because of it. I always wished she could have been a better role model and been just a little selfish. What is the point of our hard work and dedication if we can't reap the rewards and enjoy ourselves in this brief life? My outside self personifies a caring, loving, kind person, working 40-60 hours a week all my adult life. But, my secret inside self is lazy and selfish. What I want to do is, well, whatever I want to do. The last thing I envisioned myself being was in the role of caregiver.

Our Complicated Love Story

Dean and I have been together for 20 years. There have been many ups and downs, but mostly solid times bound with love. It is easy to fall into a routine, take each other for granted, point out faults in each other, and bicker about the small things. Despite these shortcomings, we recover well because we know we're committed and love each other. But what is love, really? Humans love our kids, family, pets, friends, and neighbors. We even use the term "love" when it comes to food, exercise, movies, hobbies, and books.

When I married Dean, I married a man who could be hard to love. That's not a secret; most people saw that as a red flag. I also married a man who, in five years of courtship, proved his deep desire to be a better man, to worship God, and to rebuild his family relationships. I would never try to change a person, but I was intrigued by his continual attempts at remaking Dean Faust into the man he truly wanted to be. At the same time, I saw the reflection of change in me, so we grew together. Thank God I didn't listen to other people with "good intentions." The last thing I wanted was a flatlined marriage. Lack of growth is a significant symptom of a failed marriage. I had already been through one bad marriage and had no intention of finding myself in the pitfalls of another.

Dean's biggest fear was a third failed marriage. His first two were painful and scarred him deeply. Call me crazy, but I was determined to take him on, the nurturing side of me. I wanted to prove to him that he was a loveable man and not all wives were evil. I promised to honor our vows and never, NEVER, ever leave him, nor intentionally hurt him. That is a bold promise, but I honor my promises and would drag myself through hell before breaking a promise. That promise has saved our marriage a few times over.

It has not been an easy road. We have had our share of fights, disagreements, and times of silence. Dean's fierce side can raise its ugly head but believe me, I am no princess. Dean might argue that. I am strong-willed and pig-headed, and I hate to lose an argument. That particular trait landed me in jail once. (Read book 2 of The Lemonade Stand, chapter 15 for that story). I fight ugly too. Thankfully, we are older, wiser, and, quite frankly, done with all of that. Sometimes I wonder how many marriages don't survive because they can't get beyond an ugly patch.

I didn't fall in love or grow into it over time. I chose love. I made a choice to love Dean, one that still holds today. However, my husband tells me he is IN love with me. He reminds me every day. While I am one lucky lady in that, it also renders a little guilt in me.

Choosing to love is a powerful way to love. It's not controlled by body urges or folded neatly into place as time goes on. Choosing to love is an act of commitment, a decision made equally by rational thought and emotional feelings. I would like to tell my husband, "I am so IN love with you." But I'm not sure what that feels like. I am rational to a fault, so I'll stand by my belief that making a choice to love him is equally or more powerful than being IN love with him. I wake up every day with a choice to make. It's a bit like a daily renewal of vows. I'm not here because I have to be; I am here because I choose to be.

In all honesty, these past few months post-op have challenged me like never before in our relationship. I'm not always proud of how I've handled things. But every day, I rewire my way of thinking just like Dean's brain and nerves respond to physical therapy. Am I caring for him out of duty? Yes. Do I wipe his butt because he is my husband? Of course. Do I get impatient, tired, and resentful because it is hard work and I didn't sign up as a caregiver? You bet.

My Definition of Love Continues to Evolve

These experiences have redefined how I see the meaning of love. Love is physical; even tender touches count. Love is respect and consideration at all times – not just when it is easy. Love is a commitment to do right by each other. Love includes refocusing on the small triumphs and sharing them, as hard work is best celebrated together. Dean's recovery is my recovery.

I reflect on how Dean's life could have been snuffed out in a minute's time. While my prayers have always been for his survival, I've had fleeting thoughts of what would happen if he died. Would my life be easier? In the short run, maybe; however, in the long run, it would be devastating. Who would I share those moments when we reached our lifetime goals? How would I handle the loneliness? Every day I see women around me who are alone. Without Dean, I would have no one to love, I repeat, no one to love with all my heart and soul.

What is Love, Actually?

Love is patient, love is kind. It does not envy, it does not boast, it is not proud. It does not dishonor others, it is not self-seeking, it is not easily angered, it keeps no record of wrongs. Love does not delight in evil but rejoices with the truth. It always protects, always trusts, always hopes, always perseveres. - 1 Corinthians 13:4-7

It is also about sharing common goals, honest communication, shared laughter, and good-natured teasing with your partner. I love a good laugh after an accidental snort or letting a fart go with a sneeze. Love means helping each other out without question. It's a willingness to go to the depth of your own pain, frustration, and fatigue to do everything you can to help your mate survive and thrive. Sometimes you need to let go of dreams.

Balancing work and caregiving is not easy. A couple of weeks ago, I embarked on a business trip to the United States with much trepidation. This would be the first time leaving Dean alone after the surgery. When the plane landed on US soil, I received a phone call from my neighbors that Dean was unresponsive and was taken to the hospital by ambulance. I dropped everything. At great financial expense, I immediately purchased a ticket back to Panama and made it to the hospital 30 hours later.

As I share my story, I am reminded of how love is unconditional. I first learned about how unconditional love is affection without limitations from my grandmother "Nina." She was unflappable when it came to loving her family. She was forgiving, patient, kind, and completely non-judgmental. She believed strongly in her faith in Jesus Christ and lived her beliefs. What she taught me about unconditional love is such a gift. To make up for literally stripping my husband a little naked here in this chapter, I'd like to say, "Dean, I love you unconditionally."

What the Future Holds

Where do we go from here? Honestly, I don't know. Dean faces another surgery on his lower lumbar spine as soon as he is six months past the first surgery. I'll be expecting the best and prepared for the worst. While waiting for surgery number two, we are considering some mini vacations. We hope to have visits soon with kids and grandkids, finish real estate projects, and work hard on physical therapy to get to the best physical version of Dean we can. Life is short, and there is still much to see and do.

Still on the horizon will be traveling farther and wider to places on our bucket list, as many trips as God has in his plans for us. Meanwhile, I continue to work, all the time questioning my purpose. I know my why and my passion, which is storytelling. But I am learning along this journey that God may have a different purpose for me. For the first time in my life, I am okay with that.

I learned to find joy in caregiving. I won't give it a nano-second of thought when I am called upon again. There is a beautiful purpose in helping another human being heal. Every day we are filled with gratitude. I see the blessing in focusing less on the future and instead embracing each day for all its goodness and challenges.

Life, in general, can be topsy-turvy. Sometimes that lemon tree seems to drop buckets on you again and again. When you think you've made all the lemonade you can in a lifetime, that bitter fruit invades your life with another pitcher of lemonade to make. This time, the lemonade pitcher was filled with unconditional love, proving that all you really need is love.

Michelle Faust

Michelle Faust is the founder of Lemonade legend, a company offering both print and media exposure through an anthology series, digital magazine, a publishing house, podcast, virtual stages, and Legendary Leaders TV show.

Her mission is to give people a voice, share their stories, and elevate them above the conventional noise. There is power and healing in storytelling, and Michelle's platforms celebrate the voice of individuals who have tackled lemons and created exceptional versions of lemonade opportunities. She uses a unique approach to elevate the message and the brand to optimize growth and impact.

She is passionate because of her own story and has witnessed the healing and growth that happens when people share their stories. It's an opportunity to give back by inspiring others to stand in their strength and join a community of sharing in a safe place. For most, this is where they can leap out of their fear, build confidence, and find self-love. Personal growth generally leads to professional growth as well. Michelle wants people to succeed for all the right reasons.

www.lemonadelegend.com
michelle@lemonadelegend.com
www.facebook.com/groups/LemonadeLegend
www.facebook.com/Lemonade.L.Publishing

Shattered Ideals

by Akachi Phillips

One event stands out in my childhood memories. We lived in a hilly town called Enugu in Southeastern Nigeria. Like many other families, we practiced Christianity, imported through American and European missionaries who often held open-air crusades. I was at one such crusade with my mother. Many children gathered together and sat on the dusty floors outside in the cool evening. I vividly remember it was just the children; there seemed to be a sea of us, different shades of brown skin sitting side by side as the evening went on. The adults were meeting in a different area. We listened to songs about Jesus and watched a short Jesus movie on the huge projector set up outside. Of course, it was the white Jesus; I had never known any other kind.

I was fascinated and intrigued. I watched and listened with an intensity that belied my young age. All the kids around me were quiet, and I assumed they were just as captivated as I was. At the end of the Jesus movie, one of the adult organizers stood up and excitedly and loudly summarized what we had seen and heard. The songs and movies had wet the fields, and his job was to guide us through the narrow path, that narrow door that many would not find, and ensure we made it through it. Our final destination, the promised land, heaven. As he concluded, he screamed, "how many of you want to go to heaven and meet Jesus"? I jumped up, screaming as loud as he had, "ME, ME, ME,

ME"!!!!! I thought all those other enthralled kids would be up there with me, jumping up and down. We had all heard the same songs and watched this fascinating blond-haired and blue-eyed Jesus – different from anything we saw in our daily lives. Surely they were just as excited as I was. But I was the only one jumping up and down, and all the other kids around me seemed to shrink into the dusty floors as they looked at me like some sort of strange being. Sadly, that is where my memory of this event ends. I don't remember if I got scooped up and praised by the adults for my exuberance or if I slunk back down in shame, but that event lives in my memory and epitomizes one of my childhood traits that followed me to adulthood. I did everything with full fervor. When I'm into something, I'm all in, all the way; no stops along the way. I'm not very good at doing things halfway. Once I commit, I jump in and then leap up and down and often will not see warning signs or listen to caution in the midst of my excitement.

My mother had become a born-again Christian, and as a child, her faith became mine. Church on Sunday mornings and evenings, bible study on Wednesdays, and prayer meetings on Fridays. I didn't truly understand what being a Christian meant, but I knew I was one. We were saturated with stories of heaven and hell in almost every gathering. The contrast was so stark. The horrors of hell petrified me, and I craved the streets of heaven, paved with gold, where there would be no pain, sorrow, or hunger but, more importantly for me as a child, no more flies and mosquitos!! I hated bugs, and we had plenty of them in Enugu.

Years later, in my teen years, I made a personal commitment to become a Christian, and like everything else in my life, I was passionate about church and being a good Christian. I had been a "good" girl and did my best to live by the tenets of my Sunday school teachers and the preachers. The seeds that sprouted in my faith were planted as a child. They took root in the core of my soul and centered me, a foundation that would be my saving grace several years later as life's floods swept through my life.

I was a precocious child. I loved to read and daydream. Of course, in 1980s Nigeria, I wasn't exposed to many African authors in elementary school, so most of the books I read were by foreign authors. I remember the Dick and Jane series, Aesop's fables, and collections of stories from Europe. In most books I read, families consisted of a mom, a dad, and two children. However, around me, nuclear families were larger, often consisting of a mom, a dad, and at least four kids. Some families had one dad, two or more moms, and many more kids. I felt different and special, like the kids in the books I read – my nuclear family was just my mom, dad, brother, and me. I saw my father treat my mother with love and kindness, and she loved him. My world was perfect until one day, and then it wasn't.

It was a complete and unexpected shock to me when my parents separated around the age of 8, and I found myself living with my father and brother in a different city while my mother lived elsewhere. No one ever explained why; I didn't find out why my parents separated for another ten years. The pain was excruciating, the confusion even more debilitating.

However, you didn't or couldn't ask questions during those times. I didn't know what was happening, but over the next year or so, I saw my mother go from enjoying a husband who met all her needs to having to provide completely for herself, and she wasn't doing a great job of it. It wasn't because she didn't want to or didn't have the skills, but she was an educator, a teacher, and teachers got paid next to nothing and often went months without receiving a salary. My father's job as a banker had been her shield, but now she was left without her covering, and sometimes when I visited her over the weekends, she wouldn't have enough and sometimes went without a meal to buy the special foods or snacks I liked.

I buried my pain and lost myself in my world of books, silently resentful of my father, and swore two things. I would never get married, and I would never be financially dependent on a man.

I reneged on the first and kept true to the second.

To keep true to becoming financially independent, I knew I had to be the best at whatever I did. This fit right into my personality of doing everything completely and with total enthusiasm. I had always been slightly serious-natured and smart, but I was determined to stay on top, so I worked extremely hard to achieve that goal and did so, excelling and staying at the top of my class throughout my education. I was focused on success, way too focused for my age and for the times in which I lived. My life was serious and well-planned out. I had plans A, B, and C, none involving marriage. Plan A was to become a medical doctor by age 22. Plan B was to become an economist with a Ph.D. at age 22, and Plan C was to become a best-selling author by age 22.

I graduated at the top of my class as valedictorian and got admitted into my first college of choice for medicine - a college in Southwestern Nigeria. At the time in Nigeria, graduating high school students who wanted to continue to college had to take a college entrance examination called JAMB - Joint Admissions and Matriculation Board exam. Individual universities would set their minimum cut-off scores for different departments and fields of study. Successful applicants were those that exceeded the minimum cut-off scores, and they would usually receive the score results in the mail. I was excited when I received my score results; I had applied to colleges far away from home and was looking forward to the freedom. However, weeks later, when it was time for registration, my father and I arrived on campus, but my name was nowhere on the list of admitted students. The system of notification was very rudimentary - the admitted students' names were printed in alphabetical order, with the last name first. The list was posted on a wall in the respective departments, protected behind a locked screen so that angry or disappointed students wouldn't rip them apart or deface them. I remember going down the list repeatedly and wondering why my name wasn't there. My first and last names were very long and unique; it was improbable that I would skip over it. My father went in to speak with someone in the admissions office, who insinuated that my name didn't make the list but could find its way back on the list if we were willing to do something. We drove home. I sat silently in the front seat, tears streaming down my face while my father raged about corruption and tribalism in Nigeria while promising me he would solve the problem. Weeks later, I was back on the road with one of my father's colleagues and friends who had some contacts at the university. This time, we were told that my name could get back on the list if we were willing to contribute to the department. I would be admitted into the College of Health Sciences and then transfer to the College of Medicine in my second year. In other words, I could bribe my way back onto the list. This experience was my first major moral crossroad as a young woman. I had never had to deal with serious questions of morality or right and wrong because I saw things in a very black-and-white way. Most teenagers of my day struggled with temptations such as cheating in school, lying, or hiding forbidden boyfriend/girlfriend relationships. I didn't have much of such, but now I faced a tough decision. Going to medical school was my dream. I had worked very hard to make it happen, but what I had earned had just been stolen from me. I could take it back even if it meant I had to be at peace with bribing someone. After all, it was rightfully mine. The core of my Christian convictions rose and rebelled. I couldn't do it, mostly because I was afraid that someone in the future would look at the records and expose the truth, and I would be labeled a fraud. I was very proud of my secondary school accomplishments and the discipline it had taken to get there. The thought of any of that coming into question was non-negotiable for me. So I rejected the offer to take back what was mine. My father's friend was perplexed; needless to say, the drive back home was very uncomfortable. My father was livid, and this experience marked another turning point in our relationship.

I ended up in the College of Health Sciences at another university in Nigeria. After graduation and the mandatory year of service to the Nigerian Government, I found my way to Chicago, IL hoping to continue to medical school. I was still holding true to my 10-year-old self's persuasions that I would never get married, but secretly I was a hopeless romantic. I believed in love but lived it in my fantasies and through the pages of books that I read. I had no relationships while in college; my drive to succeed overtook all. I had the same plan for my life in America, so I wasn't looking for love. I had been taken advantage of but had no experience with mutually positive relationships. I didn't know what it was to have fun or be loved. But not long after arriving in the United States, I met and married my husband.

I married for "love" and swore that my children would never experience the pain I went through as a child. My family was not overly excited about my marriage. They had so many questions; there were so many red flags. Coming from a deeply traditional society, he didn't even take the basic steps required of a man asking for a daughter's hand in marriage. Why the rush? How well did you know this person? Why not wait? Get to know him better. Focus on your studies. But I was in love. I dove right in, completely and fully submerged. I jumped up and down in excitement. Love would conquer all I sang. Divorce would never be part of our family lexicon, I declared. And so I dedicated my life to having a successful marriage and home and being present. Like most marriages, the early years were good. We had dreams; we would build successful careers and businesses. I'd always wanted to travel and see the world. He was older, more experienced, and promised to show me the world. We started a family with two children within the first four years. I gave up my dream of going to medical school. We couldn't afford it anyway, and at the time, I didn't know that loans were an option. There were no loans for college in Nigeria, and I assumed it was the same in America. I settled into working so that I could help support our family. I excelled in my career, working hard and tirelessly in and outside the home. I started a business in addition to my full-time job, and within a few years, I was the main provider of our family income. My drive came from a constant fear of not having enough to care for my children. The memory of my mother's lack and inability to provide the things I wanted was constant. I also went through periods of want when my father remarried, and our family grew. I worried that if I failed at providing for my children, they would be forced to consider and maybe even take paths that would harm them and lead to regrets. So I prevailed, driven by a deep fear I never shared with anyone. I made sure the children stayed engaged at school and in extracurricular activities. I ran myself haggard. I often worked seven days a week with my full-time job and business. I worked a full-time night/weekend shift as a medical sonographer on Fridays, Saturdays, and Sundays from 7 pm to 7 am. During the week, I ran a staffing company and provided temporary sonographers to local hospitals and clinics. Often when I couldn't find a sonographer to cover a shift, I would do it myself. Most days, I could often just grab a few hours of sleep before moving on to the next shift. I fell asleep while driving so many times; it's a miracle I only wrecked my car once. It was a Sunday morning, and I had just come home from working the night shift and was on call that morning. As I raced back to the hospital in response to a call back for an emergency room patient, I must have fallen asleep and hit a curb, or my tires blew out. My car waltzed over the median of the freeway, flipping over the barrier and settling on the shoulder. The car was totaled. I remained whole on the outside but hopelessly broken on the inside. I continued working like a maniac.

I had taken on the entire weight of carrying my family on my shoulders alone. I was never bold enough to demand more from my relationship and partner. Over the years, I'd built up a dependence on myself and never failed myself. I could overcome challenges alone and trusted what I could do, but I didn't trust my partner, who allowed me to bear it all. My resentment grew, and my marriage slowly withered. We fought about money, chores, family visiting or staying, and the children's school and extracurricular activities. We forgot how to talk to each other, and our words became weapons to hurl.

There was never any physical infidelity in my marriage, only financial infidelity. There was never physical abuse, but the verbal assault was consistent. The words cut deeper and hurt longer. They still sit in my mind, in my head, swirling around sometimes and refusing to be quelled. We both yelled at each other and said destructive things to each other. We tried counseling for years. I would start hopefully, and just as quickly, my hopes would be dashed. We tried counseling with our Nigerian Pastor and church, and when that didn't stick, we tried with our American pastor and church. Neither worked. Both parties have to be willing to do the work.

I maintained the belief that marriage was forever. I hated the word "divorce," still do. Down in my heart, I was a hopeless romantic who truly believed in forever love. I was so focused on keeping my home intact and shielding my children from the pain of divorce that I lost myself. Maybe we would be okay if I kept working harder to care for the children, the home, and the bills. Maybe things would get better if I stopped asking for help or demanding that he be involved at home and take the children to their activities. Maybe we would be fine if I worked harder and made more money. Maybe if I supported every business idea he had emotionally and financially, he would find a purpose, and things would improve. Maybe. Maybe. Maybe. I stopped dreaming. When my marriage became a wellspring of arguments, fights, and verbal abuse, I retreated, angry and miserable at home but ever the picturesque image of the perfect family on the outside. I became so good at pretending – walking into church together, sitting next to each other but not touching or speaking to each other. I remember one afternoon when one of his friends visited our home. At the time, we were not speaking to each other. Minutes before the guest walked into our home, we were shouting at each other and slamming doors. Once the guest arrived and sat down, our alter egos emerged – the perfect couple. He sat and chatted with his friend, cracking jokes and laughing, while I hovered, serving drinks and snacks, answering calls of "baby, can you bring us another glass, please". I hated myself. I wanted to scream – this is a farce!! But I had lost myself so hopelessly and long ago that I didn't know the way back.

I never shared my struggles or asked for help. I never told my mother, brothers, cousins, or most of my friends. There was only one friend that I shared my struggles with. For some reason, I thought I needed to "protect my marriage" and not wash my dirty linen in public. But looking back, I was ashamed. Many of our problems and arguments stemmed from financial irresponsibility, but I never wanted people to think he was not providing for his family. I suffered but sought to keep him protected. I still don't understand why. I think that in my marriage, I was the one who loved more, cared more, and gave more. I had more at stake because my parent's separation had brought me a lot of pain, and I had more to lose because I had drawn lines in the sand that I would not let my children experience. So I stayed and kept on.

There were many final straws, but the one that brought it crashing down was the realization of a harkening back to my life as a teenager. Our daughter's relationship with him was dismal because he had been absent even when present. He had caused her a lot of pain. As a teenager, my relationship with my father was one-sided. He loved me, but I blamed him for my mother's situation, so I loved him less. As a result, I wanted nothing to do with him as soon as I could get away, and college provided that freedom. I only applied to colleges far from home and rarely came home during breaks and holidays. My father lost me. And I lost him and my brothers. By the time my teenage and young adult years were over, and I realized my errors, I had missed out on valuable years and experiences with my father and siblings that I could never get back. They were gone forever, and I grieved them.

Our daughter wanted to get away from home and applied to colleges far from home. I knew that if nothing changed, I would lose her. I had already lost myself in the sham that was my marriage. I couldn't lose my kids.

We lived as strangers in the same house, barely speaking to each other and sleeping in different rooms. Our teenage kids saw and imbibed all these. Finally, I realized I was destroying them in my quest to protect them from the "D" word. What example of marriage was I presenting? What was I teaching them about resolving conflicts? The fights were constant, and the weapon of words was getting sharper and more destructive. We all retreated daily into our rooms, and the tension was a constant cloud. I called the kids to a meeting and told them I would ask for a "D." I apologized, cried, and explained that I never wanted it to be this way. I never wanted to be that family that others looked at in pity, especially those in the church community, a setting we were very familiar with. They both looked at me as I cried. One drew closer and held me; the other joined. We held ourselves for a few minutes, and then one said, "I'm sorry to tell you this now, but I will tell you that you should have done this years ago while I was in middle school"; the other said, "you have been unhappy for a long time." I cried some more.

I dreaded telling my mother. She was a strong Christian, and I knew she detested divorce because the bible gave no allowances for divorce except for adultery. And there was no adultery in my marriage. I remember vividly telling her as we stood outside on a cool evening. Her response floored me. I probably would have found myself on the floor if I was not leaning on my car in the driveway. My dear mother said, "I've seen you struggle all these years. You cannot force people to do what they do not want to or be who they do not want to be." I cried again. I cried a lot those days. It seemed like everyone around me was aware of the gloom I lived in, and they all knew that I needed to extricate myself from it. On the other hand, I thought I was protecting them by staying put. Everyone except me saw the cage I had walked into and knew I needed to get out.

I struggled with my faith, the bible, and understanding that God hates divorce. But I was living a deceitful life. I had no respect or love for my husband. I was lying to the church and the world. Our church periodically had evenings where couples were invited to dinner with the pastor and other church leaders. The old me would have accepted the invitation and attended the event, putting up an Oscar-worthy performance for the world to think we were the perfect couple. But I'd had my fill. Events and incidences of the last couple of years had wrought so much pain on me, the children, and extended family members. I finally had the courage to tell the church that I was done. Yes, we had been in counseling with the church, but even in that, we were not fully honest or allowed to be fully honest. I had wanted the counselor to tell my husband, "if you don't get your crap together, she's going to leave you," but church counselors do not threaten or pass along threats of divorce. So my response to that dinner invitation was, "thank you for the invitation. I will not be attending the dinner. Unfortunately, our marriage is not solid at this time, and it would be insincere for me to be present at the event". It was a turning point for me. I had just openly declared to the church that my marriage was broken. I turned to God and asked for forgiveness many times. I couldn't forgive myself for realizing that my marriage was over or deciding to end it legally. I didn't feel forgiven; I felt guilty.

I had many exercises with myself where I tried to convince myself that the future could be different. We would be empty nesters in a few short years, and we could focus on ourselves. That thought filled me with dread. I was terrified of an empty nest with just the 2 of us. And it saddened me. I cried and finally started seeking attorneys. The process was quick - it took just a few months. I couldn't bear the thought of a long and dragged-out battle, so I gave up a lot and asked for naught.

It has been two years, but many people still do not know. I guess I'm still ashamed. Maybe it's my faith or the fact that divorces and broken homes dot our national landscape, and I tried hard not to be part of that statistic.

It's been two years, and I still cringe at that D word. It's a big deal to me. So while I have no regrets that I am divorced, I have regrets about my divorce. It was never supposed to be in my life. My parents separated when I was eight, and I swore I would never go down that path. My marriage would last forever. My kids would not live with the pain and all the other unfortunate events I blamed rightly or wrongly on my parent's separation. I worried incessantly about what it would do to my kids, but I tell you that today, the kids are alright!!.

This past summer, on a hot and humid Texas evening, I was getting ready to hop into the shower and looking for music on my phone to accompany me. As I flipped through Spotify and found Lionel Ritchie, I decided to look at photos on my phone. We had just spent the entire day on Canyon Lake, and I wanted to see what we had captured. One stopped my sliding fingers as I swiped the pictures from right to left. My hand froze in mid-air, inches away from the creased screen and my eyes uncontrollably welled up with tears.

It was a photo of my two teenagers – sitting on the padded cushion chairs on the boat, side by side, skin touching, having a conversation. It was a spontaneous moment; they were unaware I took a photograph. My daughter's left foot is on the deck, her right foot resting inches higher on the chair. She's looking away from the camera, her index and third fingers splayed apart as though she were informing someone it was two. She had a smile, her right dimple clearly visible and accentuating her gorgeous chocolate cheekbones. Her brother, seated next to her, was in full grin mode. His smile stretched across his face, left to right, rows of teeth perfectly lined and visible. His smile was full, complete, and uninhibited; eyes squinted as they strained under the pull of all his facial muscles that made the smile happen. In its current loose, unruly twisted curls, his hair was the perfect top off. His fists were clenched but not in a combative fist. It was a celebratory fist; they may have been discussing his nearly successful attempt at tubing on the lake.

It was a perfect photo – beautiful, spontaneous, and with the perfect backdrop of the brightly optimistic Texas skies.

Why, then, did it bring me to tears? I have worried about how much I may have messed up my children. For years, I stayed in a broken marriage because I was determined my children would not be products of a broken home. I put up with the unimaginable and dared not to question or demand better because I was worried about the impact a "broken" home would have on my children. Even as I found the courage to change my life, I wondered and worried about the effects on my children. I worried about their mental health and hounded them to go to therapy.

Today, being away from home, taking some time to breathe and just be, I saw my children in the light of what is. They are happy, well-adjusted siblings who love each other. I did good!! They were good!

That photo was a passing moment, yet not passing. It was ingrained in time, a snapshot of spontaneous joy. Yes! The kids are alright. The kids will be alright. They are loved by a mother who has an undying love for them and surrounded by family and friends who will love them without question.

As for me, "D" was a word I never thought would apply to me, and while my life is unquestionably better, richer, and more peaceful today, I wish I didn't have to take that path to get here. I had more at stake because of the boundaries I had set for myself. But I'm learning to be free and forgiving to myself. I'm learning to rest and have fun. I'm learning to share my pains and struggles with others; I don't have to be strong all the time. That's still a hard one, but I'm trying. I'm building another business and planning to travel the world. I still believe in love. I'm still a hopeless romantic, and who knows what other journeys I'll embark on. And when I find it, I'll jump in, all in and fully submerged.

Yes, mom is alright too.

Akachi Phillips

Akachi Phillips is an aspiring writer whose love for books began in the hilly city of Enugu. As a kid, she often hid under a bed in a dark room with a flashlight to finish a novel uninterrupted.

She has worked in Women's Health for over a decade but is on her way to achieving her lifelong dream of becoming a bestselling author.

Akachi is a fearless lover of life and people and wants to share her gift with the world through her written words.

Her life and professional experiences give her a unique voice to tell stories, especially those that impact women. She is an encourager and is currently working on a platform to teach women, especially immigrant women, how to manage their money and achieve financial independence.

Akachi currently lives in Texas, always ready for her next adventure.

Email: akachi@brickandarrow.com
IG: @brickandarrowretreats
IG: @tellmymoney

Plan B to Happy Me

By Rebecca Callahan

I don't know if people have a Plan A or if it is just natural to start forming one at an early age. I had heard of young girls planning their weddings or envisioning who they would marry. I do not recall ever doing that. My childhood was more of a reaction to what was happening at the time. I just went with the flow because I was young and had no choice.

We moved around a lot when I was younger, but I grew up in the Midwest, primarily Indiana and Illinois. I went to eight schools before graduating from high school. My mom was a single parent, even when she was married. She married three times. She got married two times for sure, but the other may have been a "significant other." If you asked any of my siblings, they would agree that we grew up without dads. My mom was both our mom and our dad. She had dropped out of school after 9th grade and began working. Her goal was always to ensure we had a roof over our heads and food on the table.

A little about my mom: we will refer to her as Maggie de Indiana. An inside joke. When she would call Texas, she would speak very loudly because back then, she felt you needed to do that when you called long distance. She would always say, "Es Maggie, Maggie de Indiana!" It just made us laugh every time. My mom was fabulous. At one of the first psychic readings I had, my mom came through and said that she did not deserve to be put on the pedestal I had her on. She was wrong—she deserved that and much, much more.

It is funny how your mind plays tricks on you. I had always believed my mom dropped out of high school because she had to. I thought her dad had passed when she was a teenager, and she dropped out because she had to get a job to help raise her siblings. After all, her mom did not work. A couple of years ago, I realized that the story I always thought I knew was not even possible. I remember visiting my grandparents when I was around four years old. My grandfather was very much alive.

I told my Aunt Rose a couple of years ago that a psychic told me my mom had two younger sisters who had passed away at an early age. My aunt told me they had a sister who died as a baby and another who died after her dress accidentally caught fire when a neighbor flicked a cigarette off an upstairs balcony. Then, my aunt told me why my mom dropped out of school and left home. My aunt believed that something had happened to my mom and that my mom felt that running away was the only option she had at the time. I always felt I had such a close relationship with my mom, but now I see how little I knew about her. Maybe it was because she passed away when I was in my late 20s, so I did not get the time to get to know her better.

After someone dies, you realize all the things you should have asked. As I learn more things, it all makes more sense. Growing up, I often thought that my mom did not have the best taste in men. She seemed always to pick the wrong guy. In hindsight, I can see that she just wanted the American dream—the nice house, a good job, the guy who worshiped her and her kids, etc. Instead, husband #1 cheated on her, sold her wedding rings, gambled a lot, and was involved in some illicit activities before he passed. He was also very handsome. A Clark Gable look-alike. His name is listed on my birth certificate as my dad, but I have come to believe he was not. They divorced right around the time I was born, but my aunt hinted that my mom may have given him some money so she could list his name on my birth certificate. A gal had to be careful of her reputation in the 1960s; he was a gambler so that payment must have been a win from his point of view. I think I remember my aunt saying it cost my mom $2,000. He never acted like a father to me, so however much it was, the money just bought his last name.

Husband #2 was physically abusive. This is the one I think may have been a "significant other." Besides my younger brother having his last name, I have never seen anything showing they were married. #2 tended bar and had two teenage sons. We were only with #2 for a couple of years, but it was long enough to rip our little family apart. I have three older siblings and one younger sibling. #2 was my younger brother Michael's dad. I remember packing up and leaving the house in the middle of the night. I think I was six years old, making Michael a baby at the time. My Uncle Emil helped us move. We spent that night at a friend's house. A few days later, I remember driving down a narrow country road with my Uncle Emil's truck in front of us. A mattress flew out of his truck, and my mom ran it over. She and my uncle stopped and pushed the mattress into a ditch while my brother and I waited in the car. This image is very vivid in my head. We lived in my Uncle Paul's basement for a couple of months until my mom could find us an apartment. When we moved into the apartment, we only stayed a short time because #2 tracked us down and threatened to beat my older brother up with a crowbar. By then, my older brother Gilbert was living with my Uncle Emil. He happened to be visiting when #2 showed up. Needless to say, we moved again to another city and another school.

Several years later, my mom married husband #3. Truth be told, I am not sure how often or how much he drank when they first married, but I recall he often struggled with alcohol and cigarettes from the beginning. There was a lot of arguing in those 20+ years, especially at night. It was always the same argument, and it always ended the same way: "You go your way, and I'll go mine." But no one ever left. We begged my mom to leave, but she stayed because we had a roof over our heads and food on the table. For some reason, husband #3 *hated* Michael and me. I am not sure why. Some of the arguments were about us.

I was 9 when they got married, and my brother was 3. My older siblings were all out of the house at that point. We lived in a ranch-style home with a strange set-up. #3 lived in the back side of the house, and we lived in the front side of the house. My mom was the go-between. If he was angry at something we did, he would tell my mom, and she would tell us. If the phone rang and it was for him, I would answer it and yell out, "Joe, phone call." He would mysteriously pick up the other line in the back of the house. If I had a friend visit, we could be in the same room, and #3 would joke with my friend but never say a word directly to me. You would never know we were a dysfunctional family unless you paid close attention. I can credit #3 with my ability to work with any personality type. It is remarkably easy to "pretend" to get along with everyone; I have had years of practice.

My older siblings are 9 and 10 years older than I am. There were about four years between husbands #2 and #3, and a lot happened during those years. My sister Alice got pregnant, dropped out of high school, and married young. She made some of the same mistakes my mom made. My older brother Gilbert moved in with my uncle and finished high school in a different city. My mom thought it safer for him to be with my uncle after #2 tried to find us. He excelled in wrestling. My sister Rachel moved in with a friend's family until she graduated high school, allowing her to live an almost normal life.

I was definitely a latchkey child. Michael was still young, so my mom had the neighbors watch him. I was an elementary student going on 16. My mom would leave for work and wake me up. I watched cartoons and ate breakfast until it was time to leave for school. Sometimes breakfast was cereal with the little coffee creamers mom would take from a restaurant. It was an example of our first milk alternative. That is why husband #3 looked so appealing. He had a house in a good neighborhood, a good job, and real milk!

When my mom was in her mid-50s, she found a lump on her breast. My mom was a hard worker, and this woman did not miss work unless she was bleeding profusely or had a limb dangling off. She said she found the lump in January but did not tell us until September. It was big. It took up most of her breast. Michael wrote her a letter to convince her to see a doctor because she did not want to go. The letter did the trick, and she made an appointment. Breast cancer. It was no surprise that she needed a mastectomy. I remember sitting with her at a table in a small cubicle after her MRI at the hospital. The doctor had a thick accent and *no* bedside manner whatsoever. He slid a piece of paper across the table and said, "We need to remove the breast." And just like that, her treatment started. She had the mastectomy, then radiation, then chemo.

Breast cancer was not as openly discussed as it is now. No one told my mom she could get a post-mastectomy bra or a special cap to keep her hair from falling out after chemo. Nope. Maybe because some of these things were not as available then as they are now. There were no pink breast cancer ribbons or pink football gear during October. At least not that I can recall. All I knew was that we punted most of the time. I ordered fake rubbery breast formations from Frederick's of Hollywood to fill the bra cavity. When that didn't work, we tried bundled-up socks. We went wig shopping and discovered that some wigs could not be curled with a curling iron. That was my mistake. I will own it. She wore turbans and sometimes just went lopsided because it was more comfortable. I don't know if she stayed so positive because she truly thought she would win the fight or felt she had to be strong for us kids. Either way, she was never a victim, and I never knew her to feel sorry for herself. Instead, she was a wonderfully thoughtful person with a heart of gold. She was always thinking of others up to the end. Remember the Maggie de Indiana phone calls? Those were to family in Texas. She would often call to see if she could send them anything and continued to do so for as long as she could.

When I hear the saying, "It takes a village to raise a child," I think of my mom. Between husbands, she had five kids to raise on her own. She made something like $5/hr working at Simmons Mattress Company. I think she was the person who inserted springs into the mattresses. She would have these white utility gloves that she taped up daily, so they were extra sturdy. She worked at Simmons for about 20 years until they went bankrupt. My mom had a strong work ethic and did not believe she needed government assistance, but she often used coupons and rebates. Five for $5 Arby's sandwiches and Kmart Blue Light Specials were our friends. We were definitely raised with the help of the "village."

Elementary and middle school were a blur. It was in high school that I started to find myself. With the help of some of my teachers, I came to realize that I was smart and picked up things rather quickly. I also realized that I really liked school. It was someplace I could go and have fun and not have to deal with the dysfunction at home. Going to college was a logical path after graduating high school. After college, I was thinking of continuing school to get my Master's degree but injured my knee climbing a fence so I put that idea on a back burner. Beyond recovering from surgery and finding a job I might like, I literally had no plan.

I decided to move to Washington State in September of 1991, where my sister Rachel and her family lived. If

I had a plan, it might have been to go to college, have a fabulous career, meet a wonderful guy, have a kid or two, retire and buy a house near the water. But I didn't. Most of my life has been a series of Plan B's. The plans you have to come up with on the fly because you either weren't prepared or everything crumbled before your eyes, and now you have to punt. Yep, I have come to realize I am a Plan B kind of gal.

I think it was August of 1992 when husband #3 called to say that my mom had dropped a pot of water on her foot. She had fractured her foot in seven places. The bones had become too brittle. The doctors decided to stop her cancer treatment for a while to heal her foot. Everything went downhill from there quickly. The cancer had metastasized. I was still in Washington at this point, and I remember husband #3 saying she had turned her neck to the side, and they had heard a cracking sound. The vertebrae in her neck had shattered. She was in a neck brace. I flew in from Washington to see her four times that year. I was still hopeful at this point that she would beat cancer.

I met a guy shortly after moving to Washington. He was in the Navy. We got engaged in May and decided to elope in August of the same year. Getting married was the only way he could get some time away from his ship to meet my mom before she passed. He was with me when I saw her for the last time in the hospital. I had taken her dentures out to clean them and left them out because they were hurting her. A priest came in to visit. I thought he was just going to say a prayer with us. I was completely surprised when I realized he was giving her the last rites. I remember looking at her, and for the first time, I saw confusion and fear in her eyes. At that moment, I realized she wasn't going to leave the hospital. The neck brace was never coming off. She was losing the fight. She went into a coma shortly after and passed on Christmas Day, 1992. Michael was there that morning and said God got the best gift that year. And he really, really did.

There was no major insurance policy to collect. My mom left me as the primary beneficiary on a $10,000 life insurance policy. I gave the money to Joe, husband #3, to pay for her funeral. I have the material items I got from my mom tucked away safely in a small box. There is nothing of value to anyone else but me; rosaries, costume jewelry, her Simmons work ID, her old cat eyeglasses, etc. I inherited a number of other items from my mom. Like her, I am strong and independent, made mistakes picking men, and got breast cancer. I did one-up her, though. I was diagnosed in my late 40s and decided to have a bilateral mastectomy. Losing a parent in your 20s makes that decision incredibly easy, by the way.

In my mid 40's, I started to feel restless. I was bored. Every day was the same. Work, eat, sleep. Every weekend was the same. Sports, see a movie and then go out to eat. In between, my then-husband played video games all day and night, and I shopped. Deep down, I was starting to realize things were not going in the right direction. We were already living somewhat separate lives, so it was not so farfetched to start doing more things on my own. I signed up for a new age class that met once a month for nine months and started to do some things by myself or with friends. I realized that while I was a good mom and wife, I was a terrible me. I had lost myself in my marriage. We went to the movies every weekend, but never the one I wanted to see. Instead of arguing, I would go and see the movie I wanted to see with a friend or by myself.

"You are an amazing woman, and you deserve someone who will treat you the way you should be treated." My gut told me something was wrong when my husband of 20 years said this sentence to me after work one day in November of 2012. It turns out we were both right! He was right because I had earned the right to be treated like the amazing woman I was, and I was right because he walked out on us the next morning. He set his wedding band on the bathroom counter, packed a bag, had a quick conversation with our 16-year-old son, Chance, and moved into the basement of one of his coworkers. I like to think my ex had a mental breakdown of some sort because the co-worker was ten years his junior and lived with his mom. I will never pretend to understand this arrangement, but it was what it was.

I am a logical person by nature. After my husband left, I spent the first couple of months feeling like I should try to "fix" our marriage. We had been married for over 20 years, and I felt there was some obligation to our marriage and our son to try to work it out. I suggested marriage counseling, but my ex did not want to work it out. He did not want to do anything. He had checked out and left me to handle most of the divorce alone. I was not angry at him. Instead, I was surprised and a little bit shocked. I always thought I would be the one initiating a divorce.

We hired a mediator to finalize details instead of dragging things out in court. We could have settled things during the first visit because I had already separated most of our belongings and finances, but for some reason, my ex was stuck on making things difficult for our son. It was just a stupid power move on his part. At one point, the mediator mentioned that he should be more involved with the documentation we submitted to the court. The mediator suggested that I was not to be left to handle all the paperwork alone. My ex responded, "I trust her; she won't screw me." Hmmm... that was his first mistake. My mother would do anything for her kids, and this apple did not fall far from the tree. The minute my ex decided that we were not worth fighting for, I decided that my son and I were. My obligations to our marriage were complete.

By the end of May, we were separated, and the house had been sold. It was exhilarating, sad, and scary at the same time. Looking back, I am glad we did not "fix" our marriage. I had settled, and the sad part was that I knew I had settled long before we decided to separate. Being comfortable was just easier. The first years were up and down. I had even suggested splitting up several times before. I had wasted 15 years of the 21-year-old marriage being comfortable. It was not even a good kind of "comfortable." This kind of "comfortable" was wearing sweatpants because my jeans were too tight.

My divorce became final in October 2013, and I was diagnosed with breast cancer in November of the same year. I knew I was going to test positive for breast cancer. The summer before my diagnosis, I had downloaded a little astrology app on my phone. I would read it each night to see what the next day had in store for me. Suddenly, in the fall, I started to get weird messages. The app would say things about how I was putting off my visit to the doctor or that it was better to be seen sooner than later. I was getting the same message pretty regularly. I started to wonder what appointment I was missing. I usually had my mammogram in November and my annual in January.

My mom passed away from breast cancer when I was 28. Before I hit 30, I was getting annual mammograms. My breasts were not big but dense, so I advocated for myself and got the okay to have annual mammograms. My appointment was on Veterans' Day in 2013. I got the phone call to come back to do a magnified mammogram. I waited for those words. It was a female doctor at Kaiser who was the one to tell me the bad news. "There is a lump in your right breast; we think it's cancer." She was so kind. My first thought was about my mom and how horribly she was told she had cancer.

I went back to the dressing room and texted Chance. I did not want to cry. A bunch of women were sitting outside my dressing room door, waiting to be called back for their exams. I did not want them to hear about my positive diagnosis. Before the appointment, I told Chance I felt I would get a positive result. I did not see or feel a lump, but I felt this was what all the messages warned me about. In fact, the messages stopped shortly after my exam. Was it a coincidence, or was my mom saying "hey"? I had also gone to play bingo a couple of days before my appointment. I often asked God, my mom, and the Universe to guide me. I asked them to send me a sign. If I was going to get a positive result, maybe I could win a bingo first. I liked to keep my miracles simple and direct. I literally won $100 on the next game. S#iT! Anyway, I texted Chance at the doctor's office and told him I had gotten a positive result. He texted me back, saying, "Mom, we will get through this together." I broke down in the dressing room and quietly cried.

The minute you get diagnosed with cancer, you are assigned a Cancer Coordinator. My coordinator was named Jane. The next six weeks were a whirlwind of tests. Jane would call me and schedule tests every week. I would get one result, and we would schedule something else. My instructions were to bring someone with me when I was given my options: mastectomy, lumpectomy, etc. I brought my friend Candy, but I didn't need to hear the options. I already knew I was going to opt for a double mastectomy. It was a no-brainer. My breasts were not nearly as important as my son not having a mom. Jane told me that my surgery would be scheduled in January and that my "journey" would take a year or more, depending. Wait, what? I was getting my breasts removed – what else needed to happen? There was possible chemo, radiation, expanders if you wanted reconstruction, appointments to fill the expanders, expander removal, and implant insertion… blah, blah blah. It was a lot, and a lot of weird things happened that no one understands or explains until you go through the process.

The easy part was the mastectomy. I did the bilateral because I had a "suspicious blob" on the other breast that they wanted to watch. I was not going through all of this a second time. So, I had both breasts removed and expanders put in. Expanders are these empty bags that get slowly filled with saline every couple of weeks to expand the skin after a mastectomy. It can take months to expand skin enough to cover a size B cup implant. Everything is dependent on where the cancer was and the amount of skin you have left. As the expanders are filled, they get hard. Imagine placing oranges on your chest and lying on the floor on your stomach. Yep, it was that hard. My blood pressure at the time was borderline high, so they gave me meds to take before the surgery to even out my blood pressure because I was going to be under for 6-8 hours. When you are home and not working, your stress level drops, and this may cause your blood pressure to lower. Add some meds to that scenario, and you get really low blood pressure. My blood pressure dropped so much that I passed out twice. Once, I hit my chin on the toilet, and the second time, I hit my side on the nightstand. Nothing is more terrifying than waking up naked on your bathroom floor after you have passed out, thinking, *Oh my God…. What if I died, and this is what my son sees when he gets home from school?* Instead of calling 911, I called my friend Mary Jane to pick me up and drive me to the hospital. When she arrived to get me, she said my lips were purple. I told her to call 911 if I passed out on the way to the car. We laugh about it today and realize how stupid, yet lucky, we were that I made it to the hospital alive.

Even though I was diagnosed in November, I had to wait until January for the mastectomy and reconstruction. Two weeks after the initial surgery, I ended up in ICU and then in the hospital for 12 days. I was unsure if it was because of the low blood pressure, if the fall had caused the blood clots, or if it was a combination of the two. I was in the hospital with a Heparin drip to help the blood clots pass. Blood clots are no joke. One night I was in so much pain that I pleaded with the nurses to let me go to the ER. The doctor on call would not prescribe more pain meds. He refused and said, "You are in the best place to be right now." So, I just clenched my teeth and pushed through it. During my 12-day stay, I gained 3 pounds a day because I was bleeding internally from falling and hitting the toilet and nightstand. When you are on Heparin but bleeding internally, your blood cannot clot, so you fill up with blood and begin to look like Violet from *Willy Wonka and the Chocolate Factory.* Your skin also gives way and separates from your chest, a little thing called Symmastia. Guess what happens to your expanders when you get Symmastia? Uniboob. Yep. One expander moved to the middle of my chest and remained there until I had my replacement surgery in September. Once I had the expanders replaced with implants, things did not get better. I had gone the aggressive route by removing both breasts and nipples. When you go that route, you have options. You can remain "nippleless", get images 3D tattooed onto your chest, or have nipples surgically made. These are not functioning nipples but mounds that always stay "at attention." I went the nipple surgery route and was HORRIFIED. Did I mention that I work in a school district? The nipples were so big at first. They entered a room several minutes before the rest of me did. Then, as if things weren't funny enough, the nipples healed and almost completely disappeared into my body. In hindsight, one cannot help but ask what is the point of that surgery if they tend to disappear? Areola tattoos come next. Again, completely optional. If the areola tattoos are not done correctly, they fade over time and become spotty. Surprisingly, a nipple tattoo is usually not something just any tattoo artist will do. You have to go to someone who specializes in it.

Looking back, I was extremely fortunate. My oncologist initially thought I would need to do chemotherapy. But, my numbers came back low enough that it would not have had much effect so that I could skip that step. My cancer was hormone-driven, so the treatment plan typically consisted of needing to take medicine that reduced hormone development each day for 5-10 years. The medication could also cause blood clots, so I had to get Lupron shots for five years to medically throw me into menopause so I could take a different medication that provided the same outcome for menopausal women.

Jane was right. The cancer treatment journey takes years, and some things continue after treatment ends. Lupron makes you feel like you have aged ten years. Your joints weaken and just ache most days. Once, the nurse put the shot in the wrong place, and I suddenly began to have issues with sciatica. Last year, I had a slow leak in one of my implants, so I had to replace it. After that surgery, I opted for the 3D tattoos because the areola ones had faded completely. The scars go from the middle of each breast to the underarm area. The breasts do not look or feel natural. Gone are the days of wearing fun bras, snug shirts, or shirts made of certain materials. The strange shape of the breasts shows through, or the implant lays on your chest like a flat pancake and cannot fill the bra cavity. I am not a small girl, so finding a post-mastectomy bra in a 40A is pretty much a joke. Here's another joke for you… so this breast cancer patient walks into an oncology office to meet with an oncologist after her first one retires, and the first thing the oncologist says to her is, "Hey, it looks like you've had an easy go of it." Hmmmmm… I hate you. Maybe "bedside manners" should be a mandatory class for all physicians! Cancer does not define me, but it has certainly left its mark.

There's a saying that goes something like "act like the person you want to be." I first heard that when I was looking for a new diet to start. It is the mentality of thinking that if you eat like a thin person, you become a thin person. I have come to realize that it holds true for many things.

Even though I am overweight and old enough to get an AARP card, I try to act and dress somewhat youthful. Hence, I feel younger than my driver's license says I am. Paddleboarding with 300+ people the weekend before Halloween dressed as a witch is on my bucket list. So, I bought a paddleboard several summers ago. I can only stand for 30 seconds before falling. I even broke my toe, falling on slippery stones in shallow water. BUT I own a paddleboard, so I am a paddleboarder. I try to always look at the bright side, yet I am acquainted with Murphy's Law. I shoot for Plan A but always have a Plan B. I believe God, my mom, and the universe have my back. Time and time again, they have proven to be present in my life. If I were to sum up my life, I would need to mention Plan B's.

My goal is to be a thinner, youthful paddle boarder who is happy-go-lucky. Hmmm…I am not quite at my goal yet, but I can tell you, since my divorce and cancer diagnosis, I have enjoyed life more in the past nine years than I had in the 21 years I was married. That person that was hiding away has finally come out to play.

Right around the time I was finalizing my divorce, the housing market began to go crazy. I had to wait until the divorce was final before I could buy anything, and then when I would find something, there would be a cash bidding war. When we sold the house, we had a $28,000 sewage line issue that we discovered during the inspection. We sold the house and lost money at the same time. I was told to use the thin person diet mentality by another psychic. "Picture yourself in the home you want to be in and let God, Mom, and the Universe do their magic." I imagined something small, on the newer end, that I could afford and live in with my teenage son. Several times a week, I would ride the stationary bike at the gym and picture the home I wanted to be in. On the last day I had to tell the apartment manager that I would need to extend my lease, I got a call from my realtor that a townhome deal had fallen through, and I could go and look at it before it went back on the market. I did and somehow landed the deal without a bidding war. Crazy how that all worked out, but it proves again that someone has my back up there.

As I said before, I am not a small person. During my marriage, I had given in to eating out and going to the movies every weekend. 20+ years of that is a hard habit to break. A couple of months after my bilateral surgery, I applied and got a position making more money. I also started to wonder if this was it. Is this all there was? I was in my 50s, with weirdly shaped breasts and joints that still felt weak. Did I wait too long? Did I just jump from one comfort zone to another? I wish I had divorced years earlier and spent more time discovering who I was. I decided not to waste any more time. Remember that saying, "Act like the person you want to be."

I have always loved the water. I grew up surrounded by Lake Michigan. Several years ago, I saw a childhood friend named Bobbie on Facebook. She had gotten knee replacements and was kayaking. I kayaked years ago at Lake Powell. It was such a good time. I swore I was going to go home and buy a kayak. But I didn't. This time around, I let myself play all the head games. Am I too big for a kayak? Will it sink? Are my knees too weak from the meds? I ignored the voices and went out and bought a kayak anyway. I even convinced several friends to buy one too. Best decision ever! It does not matter if you are big, little, athletic, or uncoordinated. It is incredibly difficult not to have fun on a kayak. Now, I am not talking about the type of kayaking where you need to have a helmet on while going 80 miles an hour down rapids. I am talking about kayaking, where you paddle on a lake with a Starbucks drink and a snack strapped onto your vessel. You paddle and then stop for a snack, a sip, and a chat. It is soooo much fun that I now own a sit-in kayak, a sit-on-top kayak, and an inflatable paddleboard. The sit-in is good for chilly water, and the sit-on-top allows you to zip through the water with a cool little splash of refreshing water hitting your body here and there. Truth be told, a kayak can also make you humble. There will be times when you may have some difficulty getting out of the sit-in kayak. An embarrassing, not-so-graceful rollout will do the trick every time. Plus, that's why God made swim shorts. Getting a kayak just made me want to do more fun stuff.

Remember what my son Chance said when I was diagnosed with cancer? He said, "we will get through this together." While it saddens me that his senior year was riddled with our divorce and my cancer diagnosis, I cannot help but believe that those learning opportunities made him into the strong, supportive man he is today. The year I was diagnosed, Chance bought me a pink leisure bicycle for Christmas. It even had a basket. People who say, "it's like riding a bike," never wore boyfriend jeans with a cuff. If you tilt the bike just right on a slight incline, the pedal gets caught, and suddenly your son is there looking over you, shaking his head, while you lie on the ground with a bike on top of you. Learning to live again comes with some humiliation but a lot of laughs. And Chance was there, laughing and cheering me on every step of the way. Once you've rolled out of a kayak a couple of times and fallen off a bike, the door that was once just cracked begins to open more and more.

As you would expect, cancer makes you realize your time on Earth is limited. One of my goals since the divorce and cancer was to travel more. I was living on a single income and was raising a teenager primarily on my own. I tried to find ways to make traveling possible. I signed up for a Chase Southwest credit card and began charging my monthly expenses to accrue points I could use later to purchase airfare. It has been years since I have paid money for a flight. I also signed up for a gaming app that gave me free rooms, shows, and buffets in Vegas. I have not paid for anything but resort fees in over six years. Little by little, I started to find ways to travel more extensively and go to places I had always wanted to go but never did while married. In 2020, right before the COVID-19 closure, my travel buddy and good friend Candy and I went to New Orleans two weeks before Mardi Gras. They do all the parades, beads, and everything you picture during Mardi Gras, but with half the crowds. I also won $5,500 at Harrah's Casino there. Thanks, Mom! I had always wanted to go on a cruise. It was fun and a little scary at the same time. The ocean is big and dark! It's funny how little it takes to find that person inside of you that got put away on a shelf some time ago.

My favorite thing now is the extended weekend trip. I love visiting friends or family in a different state for 3-5 days. It is just long enough to have fun but short enough that you still feel love for the people you visit. And it is amazing what you can do in a couple of days! Before COVID, I went on a girls' getaway to Vegas. We flew in on Saturday morning at the crack of dawn. We lost $1,200 by noon, saw Blake Shelton at MGM Grand for free, downed some crazy expensive drinks, lost some more money gambling, and flew home Monday morning. This past weekend, I met my sister Rachel and brother Michael (and wife Stacy) in San Diego. We were there for five days but were incredibly busy visiting all the tourist attractions. In the evenings, we caught up on life and told stories celebrating my mom's life. Next October, Candy and I are planning to see PINK in Vegas. Tickets and rooms are already secured. Gone are the days of the wasted weekend going out to Chili's and to a movie I did not pick. (By the way, I love Chili's, so no disrespect is meant here.)

For years, I allowed myself to take a back seat to my own life. It was after my divorce and cancer diagnosis that I woke up and realized I had wasted so much time doing nothing for me and everything for everyone else. I can still be a great mom and travel, and I don't have to be thin to have fun!

I wish that I had trusted my gut earlier. I wish my mom had lived long enough to beat cancer and enjoy her life. She would have seen that the lives my sister Rachel and brother Michael have achieved had bits and pieces of the picture-perfect dream she wanted for herself. She would also be thrilled to know I am doing well and that I did not let cancer stop me. Imagine how amazing I would be if I had made changes sooner. If someone reading this says, "This is hitting close to home." I would tell them to do Something. Anything. Think of a time when you laughed so hard you wet your pants. When you went out with your friends and lost track of time doing something you enjoyed. Then, do it again. Find that sweet spot in your gut that makes your life worth living, or maybe get a tattoo to celebrate what you love. If something feels right, do it. Don't wait so long that you talk yourself out of doing it. Be spontaneous and do what feels right. One year, Chance and I went together and got tattoos. I got a heart on the back part of my shoulder with lots of filigrees. I had a small pink heart embedded into one corner that honors my mom. Chance added a pink ribbon onto one of his arm tattoos that honors me. I am sure he would agree that the "me" after my divorce and cancer is much more fun to be around. Forget about Plan A. Plan B is the path you *need* to take. And always, always, travel far enough that you find yourself.

Rebecca Callahan

Rebecca Callahan was born in East Chicago, Indiana. Before graduating high school, she attended eight schools, which helped build the resiliency she would later use throughout her life. After high school, Rebecca moved to several different states for college, work and as part of her journey for self-discovery. In Washington State, she met her husband of 21 years.

Through a company promotion, he brought her and their son to Denver, CO, where she currently resides. Raised by a strong mother to be a good daughter, a good student, a good wife, and then a good mother, Rebecca lost herself in the process, which became evident after her husband came home from work one day and said he was leaving. The next day, he was gone. Having no family in Colorado except her son, Rebecca realized she only had herself to depend on. Three months after the divorce was finalized, Rebecca was diagnosed with stage 2 breast cancer and decided to have a bilateral mastectomy. She had lost her mother to breast cancer when she was in her 20s and had decided long ago that she would take an aggressive approach if ever diagnosed. Knowing she could not control life's events but could only control how she reacted to them, Rebecca decided to continue with her journey of self-awareness and enjoy the 2nd chance at life she was given. As a single mom making an average income, she figured out ways to have fun while making an effort to step outside her boundaries.

bcally64@gmail.com

Finding Myself

By Sharla Walhood

Why didn't my mother want me? I always believed there was something wrong with me. I would doubt myself and find it hard not to think badly about why my mother would not want me. My adoptive parents never hid the fact that my older sister and I were adopted and not blood-related, either. My sister is five years older than me and a foot taller. She was always a bully to me, making fun of me at every opportunity. I would watch my friends interact with their sisters, and they always seemed to enjoy being with each other and sharing clothes and shoes. I always wished for a twin sister to trust with my secrets and share our clothes and toys with. I wanted a sister who would also be my best friend. I knew I had half-brothers and/or half-sisters because my adoptive parents told me what the social worker had told them at the adoption agency. The social worker told them my mother had an affair, and her husband would have treated me poorly, so it was good that she gave me up for adoption. My parents even believed I might be related to my adopted father's family because he said I looked so much like his own mother. He had some brothers known for having affairs, but I will not name names. My mother even remembers catching one of my father's brothers cheating with a married woman who matched my biological mother's description according to the description the agency gave her. I would not learn until decades later how different the story was in the actual paperwork I received from the adoption agency after I grew the courage to begin the search for my biological family.

I grew up in a very loving home, though, and my adoptive parents nearly smothered me with love. Even with all that love, though, the doubts that went through my mind were always there. I didn't learn until years later that the issues with myself were due to the trauma of being adopted. I always felt I needed to be that perfect straight-A student, play sports, and join after-school clubs with the hopes of getting a scholarship for college since my parents did not have the money to help. I always felt the need to be a people pleaser and rarely performed self-care. After finding myself, I learned that self-care is one of the most important things I could do for myself. Self-care is one of the ways that helped me find myself. I had spent so many years trying to help others that I never stopped to think about my needs or what I wanted in life.

My father was a stay-at-home dad, which was not common back in the 80s. At the age of 21, he had been in a horrific car accident that killed his best friend, who had been driving them into town on a dirt road. They were hit by a drunk driver who had crossed onto their side of the road while coming up over a hill. My father was thrown from the car, nearly severed his spinal cord, and broke his neck in 13 places. This occurred back in the 1950s, and my parents let me know that back then because my father was in such bad shape, the hospital's policy was to wait and see if he survived three days before performing any procedures on him. So he lay there in a coma for three days, and because he was still alive, the doctors finally took him to surgery. He did tell me that during those three days he lay there, he could hear everyone around him and how the doctors were talking about him not making it. On the third day, they got him into surgery, and he died on the operating table for over 2 minutes. My father told me that when he died, he saw his family and friends waiting for him who had passed before him. He walked into the bright light and came out into a beautiful meadow. He said he felt such peace and love there that he did not want to leave. The colors were beyond words for him to describe to me, but he said it was more beautiful than anything he had ever seen. Then a voice spoke to him and told him that he needed to return because it was not his time yet. He told the voice he wanted to stay, but the voice insisted it was not his time and he had to go back. Then he said he was back in the operating room just like a snap of his fingers. He had a long recovery, and even though at that time my mother and he were not married, she went to visit him every day for the next year while he was in a spinal halo device that suspended him above ground and kept him from moving so his spinal cord could heal. When he was released, he needed the help of a cane to get around, and my parents learned that the accident had made my father sterile. That is why my parents chose to adopt, but it took them over a decade to finally find an adoption agency that was willing to let them adopt.

Due to his disability, the adoption agencies kept turning my parents down, and it took them 13 years before they adopted me. My mother explained to me that they went to several adoption agencies in California, where they lived at the time, and it wasn't until they moved back to

North Dakota that they finally had one say yes to them. So in 1977, they welcomed my older sister into their home, and then in 1982, they brought me into their loving home. However, my childhood was challenging because my father did need a lot of help, and my mother worked several jobs just to make ends meet. As early as I remember, I had to help clean, cook, do laundry and even mow the lawn. I cannot remember how old I was, but I remember that while learning to cook, I had to get a chair to climb up on to see the top of the stove. I even remember grocery shopping alone while my father waited in the car. He would give me a blank check, and I would walk into the Piggly Wiggly, barely tall enough to see above the checkout counter. We lived in a small town, though, and everyone knew my father. The clerks would help fill out the check, and I'd bring everything out to the car and load it up. My father taught me how to do so many things, not just because he needed my help but also because he wanted me to know how to take care of myself. Before I even had my own car, he had already taught me how to change a tire and even how to change the oil. I got my driver's license at the age of 14 because we lived outside city limits. My sister had emancipated herself at 16 and, by that time, had long since moved away. My father's condition worsened over the years, and it was not safe for him to drive anymore, so I started researching how to get a driver's license and found a loophole. It was meant to be for farming families who needed help harvesting crops and driving the farm equipment down the roads to move from one crop to another. The requirements to get my driver's license that young stated I had to live outside city limits, which we did, but it wasn't a farm. The next requirement stated that the household was limited to only one person who could drive, and since my sister had moved out of state and my father couldn't drive safely anymore, that left just my mother. Since she had to be at work well before I was supposed to be in school and did not usually make it home until dinner time, I checked that off my list. The last requirements were to take driver's ed. and pass the exams at the Motor Vehicle Department. I managed to talk my parents into letting me take private driver's ed. lessons, and I easily passed all the exams. As part of their requirements, my parents stated that I would need to pay for my gas and car repairs. Plus, they even told me to prepare to eventually move off their car insurance and get my own insurance. That meant getting a job, and so by 14, I started working because I also had to get a job permit to work that young. I was determined to have my freedom because my parents didn't have much, and I wanted to buy my own things instead of having hand-me-downs. I took pride in buying my own things and felt like that lessened the financial burden on my parents.

However, more than once, I would come home and find my father lying on the floor, waiting for help. Due to his disability, he couldn't get up on his own if he wasn't in an area that would allow him to grab onto something and pull himself back up into his wheelchair. This was before cell phones, and our rotary phone was mounted on the wall near the kitchen. I can't remember how young I was the first time I had to help him get back up, but I know it was before the age of 10, and so I had to devise a way to move him to where he could get up himself because he was over 300 pounds and I couldn't lift him to help him get up. The best way I found to help him was to get a blanket and have him roll over onto it, and then I would pull the blanket across the floor and get him to his bedroom, where he could use the bed and pull himself up, then back into his wheelchair. This went on for years before finally, one time, when he fell, he broke nine of his ten toes, and the doctor suggested that it was time to consider a nursing home. The doctor believed my father's safety was compromised since my mother worked all day, and I was in school and worked as well.

I was in ninth grade then, and I remember getting called to the office because they wanted me to say goodbye to him before he went to the nursing home several miles away in another town. All the nursing homes that were in town were full, and none of them had a very good reputation, either. So from then on, it was just my mom and I living together, which meant I was alone a lot since she still worked long days and now needed to pay for his nursing home fees. My father had no social security or help from the government because every job he'd had growing up was on farms, and nothing was ever reported, so he'd never paid into the system. The State and Federal Government denied him any benefits, and all costs fell to my mother to pay. During all this time, though, my dad always had a smile on his face for those around him. I remember asking him how he could always be so happy when life was difficult. He told me that you can't always control everything that happens to you, but you can control how you respond to it. He said there was no point in being upset or angry at how things played out in life that he couldn't control, and it was better to look at the positives and be thankful that you're alive. He was and always will be my hero because no matter how bad things got, he would always find a positive way to look at it.

At the age of 18, I got married to a military man, and we moved to Japan. I had lived in the same house my whole life up to that point, and moving to the other side of the world was a bit intense, but I loved it. Then at 19, I got a call from my mom that my dad had cancer, and the doctor said he only had about 45 days to live. The Red Cross helped by paying for my and my husband's plane tickets home so I could be with him during his final days. I spent every day at the hospital with him from the moment I arrived. He was on many medicines, including morphine, because his lungs kept filling with fluid, so he was not always coherent. One morning I came into his room, and he was just like his old happy self. He told me he knew I'd been there every day since I'd arrived and wanted me to get out of the hospital and do anything else. He promised me that he was feeling better and not to worry. When I told him I didn't want to leave him in case he got worse, he said, "Don't worry about me. I know where I am going, and I am not afraid, and you shouldn't be either." He managed to talk me into leaving for the day with my husband, and when we returned that evening, my dad was gone. It was one of the most heart-wrenching days of my life up to that point. It wasn't until I was in my 30s and working in a hospice that I learned many people on their deathbed become lucid during their final hours and will turn family away because they don't want their family to see them die. I wish I had understood that back then because I felt so guilty for leaving him that day. I held that guilt inside for so many years, and it wasn't until I attended grief support in hospice that I was finally able to release it and understand it was his wish for me not to see him go. There is not a day that I don't miss him, and I wish I had gotten more time with him.

After his funeral, my husband and I returned to Japan and continued with our lives. Life there was good until my husband went on a temporary deployment(TDY) to South Korea, and when he returned, he infected me with chlamydia. Luckily, my annual woman's exam happened shortly after his return. He swore he hadn't cheated on me, but I knew I had been faithful, and I had never had any STD before this occurrence and knew he was lying to me. I was determined to succeed in my marriage, though, and thought I wouldn't uphold my vows if I got a divorce. After all, my parents had been able to stay married for over 40 years, and I thought I could do that too. So we tried to repair the trust, but he went TDY again and was in a war zone area, so his email and phone use were very limited.

While he was away, he asked me to check his email and delete junk mail so his account wouldn't get deleted. Within the first week of me taking that task on, he received an email from an old girlfriend of his, and of course, I just had to read what she wrote because he'd never mentioned that they still spoke to one another. My stomach dropped as I read how she missed him and had enjoyed spending time in a hot tub with him on his last visit home. I was devastated, as you can imagine, and I wanted to leave and never see or speak to him again. However, being a military wife, it would not be easy to just up and leave especially since I didn't have the money. Nearly everything in our home was mine, and I wasn't ready to leave it all behind. So I waited for him to call me, and it was nearly a week before I finally heard from him. When I told him what I had discovered and wanted a divorce, he begged me to at least wait for him to return and assured me that he realized after being with her again he didn't want her, he wanted me. I wanted to believe him, and I didn't see the harm in staying since he was gone, and it would be months before I would have to actually look him in the eyes. In my heart, though, I knew my marriage was over because he had broken my trust twice now, and I didn't want to be a fool. Once he came back, we tried marriage counseling, but it only helped long enough for us to get orders and be shipped off to Las Vegas, NV. Not long after moving there, I told him I wanted a divorce. We managed to part easily enough, and I packed my car full of my belongings and drove home to North Dakota.

It was a trying time for me, and I felt like a failure. I was such a believer that love could conquer all. I was determined to move on and tried to take my father's words to heart. I looked for the positives in my life. I got my associate degree while living in Japan. Once I returned home, I enrolled in the college there to earn a bachelor's degree in biology because I wanted to become a scientist or possibly go to medical school. I enjoyed seeing my old friends I'd left behind and just tried to enjoy my life. My mother even helped me buy my first house, and my sister helped me fix it up because it had been sold at auction due to the condition of the home. To this day, it is still the worst house I have ever walked into, and it was hard to keep the vomit down because the place smelled so bad. A hoarder had lived in the house with no family to pass their belongings to, so it was sold with the house. I was determined to turn my lemons into lemonade, so I got to work. It took months of back-breaking work to get everything out. Once we removed the junk, I then removed the several layers of flooring that had been put over the hardwood I finally found beneath. I tore everything out of the kitchen and bathroom. The only original thing I left in the house was the bathtub which I would have removed, except it was made of iron, and nothing I did would budge it. I even tried to take a sledgehammer to it, and it didn't even chip it. All this hard labor was therapeutic for me, and I used that sledgehammer to remove my frustrations on the walls next. I spent the next year fixing up that house and making it into a "dollhouse," as my mother called it. All while I was working and going to college.

In college, I met my second husband, who I fell head over heels in love with and thought was my soulmate. He was so different from any other man I'd met. He was from Ghana and had a cute accent. I was attracted to his intelligence and how everyone seemed to love him. He ended up moving into my little "dollhouse" with me, and we married about a year after meeting. He finished his nursing degree and got hired by the Mayo Hospital in Phoenix, AZ, so we moved, and I transferred to Arizona State University to finish my bachelor's degree. I felt like I had made lemonade with all the lemons life had handed me up to this point, and for a long time, I lied to myself because I didn't want to see the signs that I had once again picked an unfaithful man. I did not want to get another divorce, especially since so many people warned me that he was only using me to get a green card because he was not a US citizen. I didn't want to believe that, and I tried to convince myself they were wrong, but before our second wedding anniversary, I wanted to leave. However, I ended up getting pregnant, and he swore he wanted to be a good father to his child. I was terrified to raise a child alone, and he seemed so happy that I was pregnant, and he love-bombed me like crazy. I didn't know that term then, but I am well-versed in the ways of narcissism now. We struggled financially at the beginning of our marriage, but eight years into our marriage and three kids later, we started a hospice company and built it from the ground up. By this time, I had graduated from the University of Phoenix with a Master's in Healthcare Administration and became the Administrator for our company. At the same time, he was the CEO but continued to act as a nurse to help us save money. As I was busy getting the office and employees taken care of, he was busy managing the patients and helping the clinical staff. Life was starting to improve because our business grew, so did our bank account. By this point in our marriage, I had lost count of the women I suspected he'd been cheating on me with but never could get any hard proof evidence, and he would gaslight me and manipulate me into compliance. I grew increasingly unhappy as time passed, but I also didn't want to see our hospice fail. It was thriving, and by 2019 our company was worth nearly 5 million dollars. Money does not buy happiness; the more money he got, the more women he entertained. I did not learn about some until after filing for divorce, but there were a few I learned of before, which led me to get a divorce once and for all. He was buying prostitutes, and yes, I had the proof of that to confront him with it, and his response was, "The devil made me do it." As for all the other women he didn't have to pay for sex; they ranged from some of our employees to employees that worked in facilities where our patients lived and even some of the patient's family members! His desires seemed to have no bounds, and the women ranged from young to as old as the late 50s, over 20 years older than me. I begged him to stop, and we even went to two different marriage counselors for over a year, but he was lying and never intended to stop seeing other women. After 13 years of mental abuse, it finally turned to physical abuse. In a final love bombing attempt, he'd taken me to NYC for New Year's Eve, and we stayed in Times Square and could see the ball drop from just outside our hotel. He took me to Phantom of the Opera, which had been a lifelong dream of mine since I was a child. The day he hit me, we hadn't fought the whole trip, and then he got a phone call. Someone was accusing him of paying for hospice referrals, which is illegal and could cause him and our business serious trouble. I had not known him to be doing that, but I did know he was sleeping with a group home owner who was providing him a never-ending supply of patients for our hospice, and he'd refused to stop seeing her when I found out because he said he was using her to get patients. That was his justification for his relationship with her. When he got off the phone, he asked me, "Have you ever known me to pay for patients with money?" I said, "No, but you have paid with sex." In a flash, he reacted by hitting me while his cell phone was still in that hand. We had been sitting next to each other on the hotel bed, and his fist came down on my arm just below my elbow. I was shocked and asked if he'd really just hit me. The look I got from him was the most terrifying face I've ever seen. His pupils were so dilated that his eyes looked black, and his look clearly indicated he wished to kill me at that moment. I was terrified and knew if I spoke another word, he probably would try and kill me right there, so I kept quiet, and he went and locked himself in the bathroom for over 30 mins. By the time he came out, my arm had swollen down by my wrist, and I had a pain that went from my elbow to my middle finger. I was worried he'd broken a bone. He, of course, apologized after coming out of the bathroom and then tried to be a caring husband again in a true narcissistic fashion.

From then on, I knew my marriage was over because physical abuse only worsens if you stick around. My therapist I was seeing at the time even warned me that from my descriptions of our at-home life, she was worried he start getting physically abusive with me. He is truly a textbook narcissist and has every single trait the textbooks warn about that particular behavior disorder. My therapist then had been our marriage counselor, but since he would never show up to meetings, she would just listen to me and help me with the anxiety and depression he caused in me. I digress, though, and I left a lot out of my marriage with him for this story because that could be a whole novel. I wanted to share that upon returning home from NYC, I promptly went to urgent care to see if I had a broken bone because I had bruising, swelling, and pain still days after it occurred. They asked me how it happened, and I was honest. I was hoping they would call the police on him, but they didn't. I hadn't called the police on him because I was worried he would hurt me or kill me for reporting him. By this point in our marriage, I just wanted to make it out of the marriage alive and in one piece. A positive note was that my arm was not broken, and I just had severe muscle bruising; the swelling, they said, was probably pinching a nerve which is where the pain down my arm came from apparently. I found a lawyer that week and started the process of filing for divorce. I knew if I stayed, I'd always be in a state of fear, and even though leaving him brought up many other complications in my life, I've been using those lemons to make an ocean of lemonade.

Within a year of him moving out, I started up my own real estate investing company, SLFL Corp, and have been building that up ever since. I have been a Realtor for over five years and plan to continue building a real estate empire and eventually share a more detailed version of my life to help spread awareness of domestic abuse. I am an intelligent person, and yet I never understood that I was living daily with domestic abuse for years, and it took a therapist to point out to me that my marriage was unhealthy. Once my ex moved out, I could start the healing process and find myself that had gotten lost in all those years of abuse. I am thankful for all I have learned and pray that my father is looking down from heaven and is proud I can still see the positive things I got out of such a rotten situation. I have three beautiful children who are my driving force, and I want them to learn what my father taught me. Be thankful for every day, don't worry about the things you cannot control, and always look for the positive even in the direst situation. I'll add to what my father said by saying to know yourself and perform daily self-care.

Sharla Walhood

Sharla Walhood currently works for HomeSmart as a Real Estate Agent. She also owns a real estate investing company, SLFL Corp, that manages properties and financial investments in a broader range. It includes working with properties that are not active in the MLS (multiple listing service). Her tagline is SharlaSellsAZ, and her aspiration is to grow her business profits to help others in need. Especially those that are in abusive situations and need help or knowledge on how to escape safely from their abuser(s). Sharla felt trapped for so long and understands the mental anguish from years of torment at the hands of an abuser. Spreading knowledge and awareness of domestic abuse is vital, which is one reason she shared her story in The Lemonade Stand #3. Her goal is to eventually write a book detailing more about the actual abuse she sustained during 15 years of marriage and the abuse she endured during her first 5-year marriage. Her hope is that sharing her experiences with others will help give them the courage and awareness to break free of the mental chains holding them where they are at because it can be so hard to break those chains. She emphasizes that having the support of loving friends and family around you is so important, and it's something most abusers know, which is why they ruin friendships and drive wedges between the abused and their family. Sharla graduated high school at just 17 and was enrolled in college during her senior year of high school because she had completed all the high school AP courses before her senior year. She has traveled extensively but still has a long list of places to see around the world. She loves life and enjoys the adventures that wait around the corner.

Text: 480-204-5505

The Gift of Grief

By Courtney Kaplan

"When will it get easier?" I ask myself that question every day. "Time heals all wounds", Does it? I am confident whoever said those words hasn't suffered the loss of a child. Yes, time creates distance between the loss; however, losing a child is devastating emotionally, physically, and spiritually for a mother. Unapologetically, without my faith and spirituality, I am not sure if I would be a functioning human today. The passing of my son Michael created pain and an absence in my existence. Grieving the person I was and accepting the person I am. This is my journey of transforming pain into purpose.

I am a single mother with five children. I had my first child at nineteen years old. Being a child myself, my daughter and I grew up together. My life became a series of learning moments, a crash course in adulting. I was the provider, teacher, and nurturer, all running off instinct. As a young mother, I had a significant amount of learning and lessons staring me down, and frankly, I still do.

Right out of high school, I took a certification course for nursing assistants to better provide for my little family. The medical field intrigued me, and my natural ability to empathize with others made this field an easy pick. For about four years, it was just me and my daughter Aleaha. I spent all my time and energy focused on survival at all costs. Dating and social life was a fictitious tale from Hollywood; it didn't have a place in my life.

One of my first nursing assistant jobs was at a home health agency owned by one of our family friends. A co-worker of mine suggested I meet her brother. He was new to town, just moved from Chicago, and didn't know anyone. The lonely brother from Chicago became my husband and baby daddy. He and I had four children together in five years. Yes, pregnant for four years straight. Broken TV or boredom? Neither was the case. Fertile Mertile meets the Gold Medalist Olympic swimmers team. Our two youngest children were both born in 2002, one in January and one in December. Oy Vey!

We had two boys and two girls. They were so close in age that they were like quadruplets. Three kids were in diapers at any given time. Going to the grocery store was brilliant. I had to connect two shopping baskets using the seat belt from the second cart to attach it to the front one. It was a runaway train filled with boogers, sticky remnants of spilled formula, and lost Cheerios. The screaming in harmony was the highlight of my day. Thinking back, I have no idea how I ever survived. All things considered, I wouldn't change a thing if I could. Each of us endured with the help of a bit of therapy and medication. My children were my world and continue to be my greatest gift.

As the kids grew, so did I. My career path led me through a variety of healthcare opportunities. My goal was to become a registered nurse eventually. I took courses throughout my twenties and early thirties, hoping I would one day finish. I wanted to show my kids if there's a will, there's a way. Despite the hardships and struggles, you are always stronger than you know or credit yourself. I know I have proven this true in my own life countless times. After all, it's not what you say; it's what you do.

With one failed marriage and a litter of children, our lives quickly became a reality show. It's never too late, I guess.

Looking in the rearview mirror, there are so many defining moments in my life. Relationships, career paths, belief systems, and health choices have all created who I am today. Life deals out a fair share of triumphs and tragedies. It's what we do despite them that genuinely defines us. Life dealt me any parents' worst nightmare in 2019. This is my journey.

It was a Friday morning like any other. After our morning briefing in the kitchen, my teenagers and I readied ourselves for the day. Three of my children attended the same high school, which was fantastic for us; I'm not sure if the school felt the same way. It was a week and a half before my son Michael's high school graduation. He told us he was getting his cap'n gown and graduation ceremony tickets from school that day. He said he had to work his Pizza Hut job after school but would see us when we all got home. With his motorcycle helmet buckled and firmly attached, a final flip of the face shield and goodbye he went. That was the last time I would see my son alive.

It was Friday, about 1:30 pm, on my way to my next assignment. The phone rang; it was the high school. Usually, these calls are automated calls informing the

parents of upcoming events or announcements. I
generally send those calls to voicemail, but something
told me to answer it, so I did. Sitting in my car, alone at
a traffic light, the caller begins to speak. Quickly, I
realized this was not one of those automated calls. A
restrained voice begins to speak, "Hello, is this Ms.
Kaplan?" Yes, I replied. The quivering voice continued,
"My name is Lori. I am the principal of Cimarron High
School. I'm sorry to be calling you this way. Your son
Michael has been in a motorcycle accident around the
corner from the school. We don't have many details;
only they are working on him. I am so sorry." The
sound entering my body bypassed my hearing and
landed like a boulder on my chest. She continued to
speak; however, I could not hear or process words any
further. Shock slowly began to set in; I thanked her for
the call and hung up. I looked up; the frozen red traffic
light glared at me like the eyes of a wolf on a cold dark
night. Immediately, my mouth became dry. My upper
lip was sticking to my teeth, and I could not clear the
wad of thick, pooled secretions in my throat. My fingers
felt like cold icicles while my earlobes and face began
to get very hot. The sound of my heartbeat echoed
through my head louder than my positive self-talk could
whisper.

I had enough time to grab my phone, open our family
tracking app, and locate Michael's whereabouts. He
was en route to our Level 4 Trauma Center, University
Medical Center. The light turned green, and off I raced.
UMC was about 10 minutes from my current location,
so I didn't have far to go. I immediately called Michael's
father, Charles, to inform him of the accident. Giving
him the little information I had, he and our other

children jumped in the car and headed around the corner to investigate while I headed to the hospital.

I arrived at the hospital and checked in at the security booth guarding the entrance of the trauma center. The hospital social worker guided me to the gently lit private tomb in the waiting area. Slowly, family and friends gathered in 'Quiet Room ONE' at the hospital, anxiously waiting for any updates on his condition. In between calls, I remember glancing down at my phone. I caught a news bulletin streaming from one of our local news stations. The headline read, "Crash shuts down Lake Mead at Buffalo in both directions; motorcyclist seriously hurt." An image of Michael's mangled motorcycle lying in the middle of the traffic lane with his lonely gym shoe making a front-row appearance. Both items were circled in green spray paint, waiting for someone to solve the puzzle. The bulletin continued, "18-year-old fighting to survive after the crash." It was my first clue into what awaits me on the other side of the double doors where Michael fights for his life.

All I could do to quiet the storm in my mind was to meditate. In a calm and gentle voice, Michael impressed this thought onto me, "Mom, I have to go. I know you are scared and sad, but I will always be with you, always." With that, a warm, energetic all-encompassing internal peace came over my soul. I felt his spirit flow like a soft breeze through the leaves of a tree. With that, I knew my life would never be the same, and I also knew Michael would not be walking out of this.

Two hours passed before we could see Michael. Charles and I were escorted into the trauma center. As we cleared the corner, the green curtain surrounding his bed embraced the secrets it held within. Beyond the curtain lay a set of circumstances I wanted to leave in my nightmares where they belonged. I saw my beautiful baby lying in the hospital bed with a gown gently placed over his body. His right eye had significant swelling and mild bruising. Blood dripped from his right ear into his ear canal, and his hands had minor scrapings on his knuckles. The sound of the heart monitor and breathing machine created a melodic intermission, a distraction readying me for the next part of the show. I grabbed a chair and sat as close to his bed as possible. I laid my chest across his still legs while I enjoyed his warmth and vulnerability in the coldest moment of my life.

I took as much time as I wanted and needed, holding and touching him. I played with his curly hair and kissed his cheeks like I did when he used to look up at me with his big brown inquisitive eyes. Something I knew I would never see again. I cut a few small swatches of his perfectly styled hair. One thing about Michael is, YOU NEVER TOUCH HIS HAIR! I was comfortable breaking the rules this time. I was up for the challenge, secretly hoping this would arouse a response. One never came.

The trauma physician made her way to our island of despair. We learned Michael had suffered a severe traumatic brain injury. The internal injuries to his head were extensive and worsening. Brain swelling, facial fractures, and brain bleeds continued to paint our new reality. He was stable yet extremely fragile; his prognosis left little room for hope. The physician offered her condolences and stepped away to care for the numerous traumas making their way into her daily duties. I stepped back to Michael's bedside, stealing as much time as possible before we were returned to the holding tomb. We were led back to the waiting room, where the truth awaited the rest of the family.

The following morning, we consulted with the Neurologist assigned to his case. He confirmed Michael was officially brain dead with no chance of recovery. The silence in the room was deafening. Once again, the sound of his life support gave a note to the death sentence we all face in our own way. As the doctor moved toward the door, he left us with, "I'm sorry," and vanished into the corridor. Somehow it felt like unwelcomed charity. A decision will need to be made.

Thanks to my career, I have opportunities to provide sympathies and kind words of support being in the medical field as long as I have. For those left behind, existing in a world without their loved ones can be overwhelming and uninvited. Loss is a part of life; it just is. This time I was on the receiving end of condolences and sympathies; it was now my turn. My children and family looked to me for comfort and guidance while I was slowly dying inside, clinging to life myself.

Any parent will confirm that the needs of their children come before their own needs, no matter the price. My uninterrupted responsibility to protect Michael and his interests above all else guided me through the hardest decision of my life.

A year before Michael's accident, he and I took a trip to the DMV. As much as I begged and pleaded for him to consider a car vs. a motorcycle, I lost. Michael, now eighteen, could fill out the license application and sign on his behalf. As he made his way through the application, he stopped at the section of questions surrounding organ, tissue, and eye donation. Michael asked me to explain what being an 'Organ Donor' meant. After meeting his inquisitive innocence, Michael selected YES on all related questions. I never imagined in my wildest dreams this conversation would be one of my greatest blessings.

At Michael's bedside, the family briefly discussed Michael's fate. We unanimously agreed to release Michael from his lifeless body and uphold his wishes as an organ, tissue, and eye donor. Knowing Michael would live on in the lives of others was nothing short of a miracle. Immediately, a sense of relief came over me. I imagined my life without Michael as tragic and full of grief as it will be; I also saw a life filled with hope and gratitude. Where else do grief and gratitude live in the same space? I can't answer that, only that it does. I'm living proof that it does.

A representative from Nevada Donor Network arrived in our room about an hour later. Rey introduced himself with kind words of compassion and support our family desperately needed. His words left his loving heart and landed on the many cracks in mine. He gently explained the process in terms that even shock couldn't obstruct. Rey mercifully explained that the coming days might be harsh and unbearable. Extensive testing, medical scans, and treatments are required to ensure his donations' greatest outcome. This process may take four to five days while the results are analyzed and recipients are matched. At this time, Michael's team will continue to monitor him closely and update us on the progress. With his kind eyes and unbelievably warmhearted soul, a lifeline was tossed; I grabbed on with all I had and never let go.

On day three, I asked my dear friend Ruben to stop by the hospital and pray with our family. Ruben was not only a family friend but also a gifted chaplain. He and his wife arrived in our room with swollen red eyes and saturated tissues. As I filled them in on the latest updates, Michael's nurse adjusted his IV medications. She made the adjustments in hopes that his vitals would return to a favorable figure. While his heart and lungs attempted to restore their full function, Ruben began to pray. Only his inspired words and the rhythmic beeping of the medication pumps and heart monitor could be heard. The request for a peaceful release and a plea for mercy was heard by Michael, the Almighty, and all in the room. "AMEN." Suddenly, his heart rate slowed, his oxygen level rose, and his blood pressure reduced. The nurse came in perplexed and confused at the recovered vitals. The nurse had to adjust the rate and dose of the medication pump prompting additional chest x-rays and lab work to document the episode correctly and accurately.

Rey stopped by later that day and, with surprise and wonder, stated that Michael's heart and lungs had healed enough and were viable for organ donation. All I could do was sob. We had just witnessed another miracle. The following day, Rey confirmed that eight individuals had been matched with Michael's organs. His heart, double lungs, liver, both kidneys, and pancreas. The lives of countless others will be enhanced through tissue, ocular, and bone recoveries. In addition, Rey explained Michael has blood type B. When it comes to organ donation, blood type B is the rarest uncommon opportunity. The recipient list is long, and many die before a donor match is found. I would imagine those patiently waiting on the list have prayed for a miracle with every call they receive. For those eight people, Michael was the answer.

Our story received significant local press and aired on multiple news platforms. Newspapers, PEOPLE Magazine, and CNN all covered this story. During the five-day stay at UMC, Michael's father and I conducted numerous interviews, introducing this young hero to the world. His accident and decision to be an organ donor at such a young age highlighted the importance of organ, tissue, and eye donation. More importantly, it punctuated the absence of transplant services in our state. Over 650 Nevadans are waiting for a life-saving organ and a second chance at life. Our story and the publicity forced action from our local state and federal agencies. In life, Michael advocated for those voiceless and vulnerable; why would his death be any different?

Speaking of the vulnerable and voiceless, after the accident, I quickly learned some of the details surrounding this accident. The following Monday after the accident, one of Michael's friends and classmates coordinated a candlelight vigil at the accident scene. One young man sought me out as I huddled around the comfort of family and friends. He introduced himself and said he was the passenger in the car that was involved in the accident. He was visibly upset and clearly affected by what had happened. I held him as tight as I could while he cried. He assured me he and the driver were not impaired. This accident was indeed an accident. He told me he and the driver, Vonn, were graduating seniors at Cimarron High School too. They knew of Michael; however, they were not known friends. Once I learned we were dealing with kids, it suddenly became a mission of mercy.

At this point, my main concern was meeting this 'Vonn" and finding out how he was doing. My mommy heart knew that he was suffering; he was scared, and only I could help him. Soon, I heard from Vonn's mother, Merci. She wanted to share her condolences with me and find out how I was doing. Both of us cried, knowing our lives would never be the same. She, too, was a single mom, doing her best to care for her family. She was terrified for her son's future and mourning the loss of mine. I assured her I would do everything within my power to ensure her son would have the greatest chance at living a full life if I had anything to do with it. Merci was very fearful of her son's mental and emotional well-being. He had closed himself in his room, wasn't eating much, and refused to attend his high school graduation. That was all I needed to hear. I was confident, Vonn needed me, and I needed him. I asked Merci if she and Vonn would come to our family home and let me speak with him. He was crushed, devastated, and scared. If there was to be any relief for this young man's burdened heart, it lay firmly in my hands.

Our family meeting was arranged, and Merci and her family were coming to our home. It happened that Cassie from Channel 5 FOX news had already scheduled an interview at my home. What better way to show our community what forgiveness and love looked like than to be that example?

Vonn, his mother, and his brother Sean arrived. They slowly exited their vehicle, visually distraught and emotionally defeated. I walked up to Vonn, and with open arms, I pulled him to my chest as I did with my own children needing comfort. Vonn surrendered and wept in my arms. With his mother and brother looking on, I led Vonn and his family into our home and sat them down at the kitchen table. Charles sat across from Merci while I sat to the right of Vonn in between him and his brother. Vonn's head bowed in shame, and tears poured from his face, landing like water balloons on his trembling lap. I grabbed his free hand with a gentle grip and began our healing. As Michael's mother, I told Vonn I was not mad at him. I forgive him and don't blame him for Michael's passing. This was an accident that changed both our lives forever. I was curious about his plans for the future, his immediate plans after graduation. If this accident hadn't happened, what are your dreams and aspirations? Vonn went on to describe his lifelong dream to be a heavy equipment mechanic in the military. He also shared his hesitation about attending his high school graduation. I learned he was getting death threats on social media and being treated differently by his peers at school. His shame and profound regret exuded from him.

Without hesitation, I asked Vonn to raise his head and look at me. Eye to eye, hand in hand, I thanked him for being open with me and sharing his concerns. I could see his pain and angst and wanted to fix it. I promised him I would take care of the death threats and address those concerns with the news media. At the same time, I asked him to make me a promise. I asked Vonn to please attend his high school graduation. My family and I were attending the graduation in honor of Michael, and we would be there for him too. More importantly, the greatest gift he could bestow upon me is to fight to live his life for himself and Michael. "We don't need to lose two kids," I explained. With a sympathetic nod and a quiet confirmation, he agreed. He and I were going to get through this together.

Later that day, our family returned to the hospital to visit Michael. Rey approached our family with an incredible opportunity. Nevada Donor Network and UMC offered Michael and our family to be their first-ever Honor Walk recipient. Our family jumped on this unbelievable opportunity. The Honor Walk would take place the following morning.

We invited family and friends to attend Michael's Honor Walk. I remember emotionally preparing for what was to come the best I could. Tomorrow would be the last time I would ever see my son. It's like preparing for lethal injection. You will never know how it feels until it's over. No matter what, I would be ready.

It's the morning of Wednesday, May 22, 2019. I arrived at the hospital with Michael's sisters Eden and Aleaha, his brother Christian and his father. Michael's best friend David and his family came to pay their final respects along with Michael's friends from school. Close family gathered in Michael's room for final preparations. We draped his graduation gown over his lifeless body. After all, he was a high school graduate and deserved the recognition. The nurse and attending physician began to disconnect him from the ventilator and infusion lines. An Ambu bag was connected for manual breaths. The vitals monitor was detached and gently nestled next to his body, where the monotonous beeping continued. I brought his favorite pillow for comfort and his rubber snake, which I placed around his wrist. With the bed free from the tethers of treatment, he was wheeled out of the room and leveraged for passage to the operating room.

Our family stood at the head of Michael's bed, steered by his bedside nurse and two representatives from Nevada Donor Network. On the left of the bed was the physician maintaining the Ambu bag, and on the right was the nurse reviewing the vitals monitor. Several individuals stood at attention along the wall as we cleared the first turn. Some bowed their heads, visually overcome, some shared a half smile, and others made no eye contact. As we cleared the final turn, I broke my gaze on Michael to witness the sheer magnitude of this historic event. Hundreds of people lined both sides of the hall. From my vantage point, it looked like his bed was levitating, escorted by the myriad of angels lining the passage to heaven. Some faces I recognized as UMC staff members. Others were faces of strangers bonded by tragedy and inspired by love. Michael's vital monitor beeping echoed through the hall, interrupted only by the sound of sobbing and sniffles. What felt like forever turned out to be a five-minute trek. I spent MY final minutes with Michael celebrating the eighteen years I had being his mom. I relived the moments he and I shared throughout our time together—the many outdoor adventures, our hikes, and trips to the park.

Michael and I shared a love of wildlife and a love of food. Our bond transcended this physical world. He knew what I was thinking, and I knew what he was thinking. He was sensitive to messages from the other side, a skill we share. I spent my final moments reflecting on the time we had together rather than focusing on the time and experiences we won't have together. I recalled the many bribes and pleas for a reasonable compromise surrounding his transportation. From childhood, Michael was obsessed with motorcycles. He and his father shared a love of the freedom only a motorcycle provided. In fact, a week before the accident, Michael and four of his riding friends headed to Red Rock for a bonding bro ride. Michael told his friends on that ride, "If I die on my bike, I will die doing what I love."Somehow, knowing that brought me some peace and healing. Almost like this was a mission of the divine.

As we neared the final turn into the entrance of the operating room, the hallway narrowed, and reality set in. The momentum of the bed slowed and came to a gradual stop. The nurses began to remove some of the attachments from his person. Michael's father succumbed to his grief, causing his gait to wither like the crumbling of an old building. Rey quickly grabbed onto Charles, preventing him from completing his fall. The wailing sound echoed through the hall like the chanting in a Buddhist temple. Eden and Aleaha hugged Michael as tight as they could without disrupting his perceived slumber. I laid over the side rails of the bed, gripping his hand with no intention of ever letting go. Inspired to speak his final sentiments, Charles' father began to speak to the crowd. He clutched his chest, one hand over the other, to shelter his broken heart from exposure to the pain. "If anybody can hear my voice, my baby boy made a conscious decision to do this. To share the gift of life with whoever is going to receive it. So please know we are in the presence of an angel". As he released his grip on his chest, he bent over the head of the bed to share a gentle kiss on Michael's forehead. He rose from the kiss, with one hand on his chest and one hand on Michael, and continued, "I'm so..I will never be more grateful for anything than having been blessed with being his father." With one final kiss on Michael's forehead and a gentle stroke as if to seal the sentiment. A final "I love you" quivered from his shattered heart. With a discreet nod, the medical team gripped the bed and steered him through the double doors of the operating room. This is the last time Michael and I will be together.

We were escorted by hospital staff, along with family and friends, to gather outside the hospital. We assembled in the hospital entryway, appropriately named Hope Lane. Here we were greeted by the CEO of UMC, Mason Van Houweling, and several UMC staff members. With tears rolling down his face, Mason handed our family a commissioned piece of art signed by each clinician who cared for Michael. A bundle of blue balloons was separated one -by-one and given to each of us. With a brief prayer, we released the balloon into the air, allowing the breeze to support their journey to freedom. The balloons disappeared into the horizon, and loneliness began to set in. We were leaving the hospital for the last time, never to see Michael again. It was a cold and eerie feeling.

Returning to life, as usual, seemed the best idea at the time. I took two weeks off from work. My employer was extremely understanding and accommodating. Still in shock, grieving, and unsure what to do from one minute to the next, the break was much appreciated.

It was like a dog chasing his tail at times. I needed one piece of information, yet it had to follow another piece of information that required that thing which hindered getting the right rep on the phone. Oh boy, it was tough. In the meantime, I regularly communicated with the detective assigned to Michael's case. Constantly discussing the finite details of the accident, fully engaging my ability to think when all I wanted to do was feel. I requested the accident report, picked up the coroner's report and the death certificates for the funeral handler, and arranged a celebration of life ceremony. I felt like I was on autopilot at times. Was I in shock, or was this grief? I'm sure it was a little of both.

It is graduation day. Our family prepared for Michael's graduation ceremony. A dear friend rented a large 25-seater van with a driver to escort us to the high school graduation. We made our way toward the stadium entrance, where the students gathered for the final hour with their comrades, many of whom they would never see after today's commemoration. Vonn was standing with his friend, gowned up and ready to walk. We stopped, hugged him, and snapped a family photo. He was reserved, yet there was a hint of relief knowing we were there to support him.

Our family found our seats directly behind the honored students and in front of the stage. After the customary opening remarks and the national anthem sung by one of the talented music students, we took our seats. Lori, the principal, took to the stage handing out blessings and good tidings to all in attendance. When it came time to begin the graduation walk across the stage, she paused with a powerful message. She gave notice to the tremendous loss suffered by not only Cimarron but our community. " We will always remember Michael Sigler and celebrate his heroism. She allowed Christian and me to walk across the stage and accept Michael's diploma on his behalf. Christian had draped Michael's gown over his right arm, and I was on his left. We received his high school diploma and welcomed the roaring applause and standing ovation, recognizing Michael's accomplishments and positive impact on the world. Our family left the graduation ceremony with our heads held high and hearts beaming with pride.

Like politics can divide even the most connected folks, so can death. Death is difficult for most; however, it is processed as differently as the snowflakes falling from the heavens; no two are alike, and each is unique in its own right. I had experienced loss in my life. I lost both sets of grandparents, my stepfather passed away just two years before Michael's accident, and I had lost a few close friends over the years. Four-legged furry friends had come and gone, each taking a toll on me. None of those losses I experienced could have prepared me for the magnitude of pain, the chaos, and the aftershock I experienced losing my son. Welcome to your new life Courtney.

I spent the next four months settling into my new life without Michael. I spoke about our story to many different audiences. News media, newspaper articles, and interviews were a weekly occurrence. A friend texted me a picture of his television screen. CNN reported our story on one of their broadcasts. A news outlet from Russia contacted me on Facebook Messenger asking to feature Michael's Honor Walk, highlighting the life of this young hero. PEOPLE Magazine contacted me for a featured article sharing the details of our story. Michael's Honor Walk went viral on YouTube. The busyness was a welcomed distraction. Silence was too loud for me now. I became a volunteer at Nevada Donor Network. Sharing my hope and strength with others was a huge part of my healing process. It gave me a safe place to express my grief, gratitude, and empathy for others in a similar position.

I took the time I needed to gather my thoughts and feelings surrounding Michael's absence and learn to co-exist with the vast hole in my heart that continued to ache before I took the next step of my journey.

It was mid-September, about four and half months since Michael's passing. I decided to take my grandbabies to the public library. I brought my notebook with me, something I never left home without. While I was there, I was inspired to sit down and write. What started as a journal entry quickly became a heartfelt letter to my recipient families. I started out welcoming them to our family. I needed to express my immeasurable gratitude for their extraordinary role in my life. Without them, Michael was just another tragic young motorcycle accident victim. Without them, Michael was just gone. Adhering to the specs of this type of correspondence, I was conscientious not to divulge any identifiable and personal information. No last names, no contact information, no photos, or any such details that could lead to an uncomfortable situation or inappropriateness. I began with this introduction, 'For many families that suffer the loss of a loved one, especially a child, one may understandably search for the reason, 'Why, 'Why me,' 'Why my son or daughter.' I found my answer on May 22, 2019, and that answer is YOU!" I continued, "I am filled with gratitude and honor knowing that he chose me to be his mom and lead him on his path to you."

Expressing my deepest emotions and finally connecting with that piece of Michael's light was extremely healing and gave me a sense of indescribable hope. I was not only sharing my thoughts and feelings on paper; I could potentially speak to or meet one or all of these amazing people that hold an exceptional piece of Michael. Michael was and is my baby. These individuals need to know something about the person whose life they shared. "Through it all, please know you are sharing the life of a soul filled with love and adventure, a life that loves reptiles. Michael's equally special love was his motorcycle, which he bought and paid for himself. He loved orange chicken and Oreos, not at the same time, of course".

Although I was on the donor side of life's coin, I was careful to recognize the struggles a recipient and their family may have. A common reaction for organ recipients is called survivor guilt. The overwhelming feeling of grief and sadness, knowing that for them to live, someone had to die. These feelings are common among people who survived a traumatic event when others did not. The 'why me' syndrome has different interpretations. I need to disband and debunk such fears any of Michael's recipients may experience. "My hope for you is you have found peace, love, and strength in knowing the life and struggle you may have had before your gift is only a memory of a past that reminds you how precious life is and how valuable our loved ones are. You deserve the opportunity to live your best life without the fear that your last breath or last heartbeat, or last embrace might be today. My reaching out was for myself and Michael to welcome you to our family." I signed the letter as Courtney K. I forwarded it to the aftercare department at Nevada Donor Network, and they distributed it to the various transplant centers that received Michael's organs. I was made aware it would take upwards of a year to receive a reply IF one of the recipients decides to write back. I prepared for the worst and hoped for the best. Meanwhile, I received a detailed description of Michael's organs and the age and gender of each recipient. Again, no names or contact info is shared out of respect for privacy.

Here's the information I received;

Double-Lung Male, age 61

Liver Male, age 57

Right Kidney, Female, age 40

Left Kidney, Female, age 25

Heart Male, age 18

Tissue, bone, and ocular donations - TBD

I sat with this information. I gave it time to sink in. After learning the details of Michael's recipients, during my daily routines, errands, and such, I would secretly wonder if someone in the random public around me was one of our 'extended family' members. Very bizarre. If an oxymoron could apply to emotions, this would be a perfect example. During a moment in time, the overwhelming feeling of gratitude and appreciation for Michael to live on in the lives of others, yet, my heart aches from the absence of my baby. My grief is constantly processing like an app running in the background on an electronic device. It's always there and always present.

At about the six-month mark, I took to Facebook, hoping to skip the waiting game and connect with one of our recipients. I recorded a video of me reading the letter I wrote to the recipients a couple of months prior. I also included the organ donation details and the date of donation. I asked that people share, share, share. As I've stated, Nevada doesn't have a transplant center except for kidneys. Most of Michael's organs went to one of the many outlying transplant centers outside the state. Arizona, Utah, California, and Texas tend to be regular receivers of organ, tissue, and eye donations procured out of Nevada. Despite the many 'likes' and 'shares' my video received, no one reached out.

It was Tuesday evening, August 4, 2020. I was nearing the end of my work day. Amid the COVID-19 lockdown, I worked from home more often than not. I heard a 'ding' on my phone, alerting me I received a Facebook notification. The notification was from a woman named Mallory P. from Dallas, Texas. We were not Facebook friends, nor did we share any contacts. I opened the message, and this is what I read, "Hi Courtney, my name is Mallory, and I am the daughter-in-law of Mike's double lung recipient. We just received your letter TODAY, all these months later. We found you from the information in your letter and confirmed with the video on your Facebook. We were going to reach out, but the center advised us to wait as it is hard to find the right words to say when you are given a second chance at life. My father-in-law's name is Harold, and he would love to speak with you if you are open to it. His number is XX. He can't wait to hear from you, learn more about Mikie and welcome you to our family."

Instantaneously, I began to tremble. The phone dropped from my hand and landed on the table. I was in disbelief. Is this happening? I had been hoping to contact one of our recipients for over a year. My heart began to race, and excitement took over my every thought. With Charles nearby, I picked up my phone and clicked on the phone number embedded in the message. The phone rang twice, each ring delaying the reunion with my son. I heard the voice on the phone inhale for the much-anticipated introductory greeting. "Hello," in a Texas drawl. I heard his voice, feeling his life force through the phone, knowing he held a piece of my baby I used to carry when we shared a life together. When my body housed his little life, protected him, and loved him before I held him in my arms. It was a surreal moment I will never forget as long as I live. I began to cry. These were tears from a grieving mother so moved by emotion and grateful for this experience.

Harold, Charles, and I spoke for two hours that evening. We shared the lives we lived before the accident and the lives we live now, having been thrust together, with the common bond being Michael. Harold and his family celebrated their second chance at life, while I celebrated my second chance too. I could live for Michael and through Michael, but in a different way. As we continued our conversation, it was clear both families were desperate to meet each other in person. Michael's 20th birthday was in the coming October, two months away. I suggested we celebrate Michael's birthday with Harold and his family in Texas. It would be my second birthday without Michael. What better way to acknowledge his presence and presents than to spend it with our new family in Texas?

Harold arranged airline tickets for Charles and me to travel to Texas and spend the weekend at their lovely home. I contacted Nevada Donor Network and invited them to accompany our family on this once-in-a-lifetime opportunity. They would document our experience, interview our families, and record the much-needed testimony for the state transplant center project spearheaded by Nevada Donor Network.

We met Harold and his wife Bee at passenger pick up, relying upon the description of the car that held this miracle within. Bee hopped out of the passenger front seat as they pulled up and ran to me. The embrace transcended our physical bodies and lingered in a place where time doesn't exist. Mother to mother, the touch was so tender, and supportive words were unnecessary and would have been a distraction. Meanwhile, Harold came around the rear end of the vehicle. He headed towards the sidewalk where Bee and I melted together. Releasing my embrace, I turned towards Harold. Our eyes met with his arms wide open, giving me full access to his chest; I laid my head on his chest and connected with Michael's life force. I knew I was in the presence of my baby boy. I felt the energetic connection Michael and I shared, a special part of my everyday reality. Harold allowed me to hold him as long as I needed.

During that visit, we met Harold, his wife, his only son, and many of his extended family and friends. Sitting down with them and learning about their lives before his transplant was overwhelming. Listening to a wife and son describe Harold's fragile life, realizing he was close to death due to a long-suffering chronic lung disease, gave me a renewed appreciation for our gift. His adult son got married six months after Harold's transplant. His father would have missed this only son getting married, and his son would have lost his father, unable to share such an important day with him. They lived with the constant fear of his delicate mortality. Yet, they feel such a sense of sadness knowing the sacrifice paid for him to live.

On Michael's birthday, Harold and his family arranged a beautiful family gathering, preparing some of

Michael's favorite foods and his favorite Oreo cookie cake. Many of Harold's extended family traveled around the country to meet us and celebrate Michael's birthday. Brandon, Harold's son, had a huge bundle of balloons with long strings attached. Each attendee wrote a personal message to Michael and attached the handwritten note to the end of the balloon strings. Harold led the way to the launching spot on his park-like property with the balloon bundle tightly clutched.

Clear of the trees with a gentle breeze on deck, Harold handed the dancing balloons to Michael's father, and I recorded. With Harold on his right and Brandon on his left, Charles raised his arm, gripping the balloons as an offering to the Gods, and released them into the heavens. Happy tears fell from my face like the rainfall from a summer storm. Soon the balloons disappeared into the sunset. I can still remember that day like it was yesterday. This experience connected me with a purpose, the ability to continue the work that Michael began through his selfless decision to be an organ donor. There is no greater joy or honor than to support your children and watch them spread their wings and fly. Fly, baby, Fly!

I returned home with a renewed sense of purpose. Not only did I reunite with my son on a whole other level, but I also closed the loop. There was a sense of closure, a sense of peace. The beginning of my first realization that gratitude and grief can live in the same space. It became necessary for me to explore this phenomenon. Not for me but for the countless others suffering from unresolved grief and perhaps the anger surrounding their emotional injury due to the loss. I am armed with Michael's love and the championing inferno within me. My journey is my story of tragedy, divine purpose, and finding the gifts in loss. The peace and love I have found since I lost Michael has brought me such clarity and ignited a passion, all fueled by my grief.

With a renewed passion and purpose, my professional impact was essential elsewhere. A safe place where Michael and I could support others on their journey through loss and grief while continuing to heal ourselves. Hospice and palliative care for children and adults were where I landed. Shock, disbelief, feeling alone, anger, and perhaps withdrawing from life are all normal responses. I know them all too well. Getting into the 'pit' with the families is one of the many gifts of grief I now recognize. No matter the age of the individual, reassurance and acknowledgment can make all the difference in someone's journey through loss. I can't save a life, but I can always affect one.

I can say with certainty that the person I was stopped at the red light on May 17, 2019, waiting to get to my next patient, ceased to exist at once with the power of one phone call. From that moment on, the person, the mother, the friend, and the professional I was, died with Michael. It took such a tragedy to shake me out of my life on the hamster wheel and step into a purposeful life. I fell prey to the daily grind, the habits, and a life with blinders. Sometimes it's easier and more comfortable to keep doing it the way it is than to challenge the norm and get out of the sufficient zone. Before I lost Michael, I treasured and valued my relationships. I loved my children with all my heart and soul. I was grateful and appreciated the life I had; however, through the gift of reflection, it has changed. I realize that my existence in this life is not promised, nor are the relationships and material things. I must spend time with conviction and purpose if time is my greatest gift.

Relationships are value based now. Time spent on negative and unsalable relationships takes precious time away from those that bring me joy and happiness. When you reflect on your life, do you criticize your past for its brutal honesty or show gratitude and appreciation for creating the incredibly powerful 'you'?

Without your past, all the triumphs and the tragedies, you would not be who you are today. Each experience is critical in composing the beautiful and unique artistry you are today. No one in this world has, is, or will have the craftsmanship and wisdom you bring. If this is true, then our experiences aren't good or bad; they are merely moments that we use as a reference for creating our future. Accepting and embracing the power to choose our memories' meaning is a game changer.

Our lives consist of a series of precious moments. We attach meaning to these moments, creating an experience we file away as a memory. As I reflect on my life, all the moments are tucked safely away.

I can recall finite details surrounding that moment or memory from the room's sounds, smells, clothing details, and feelings. The call I received on May 17, 2019, will forever be a part of my narrative, down to the finest detail. My thoughts, feelings, awareness, and beliefs all have a permanent record in my journey. Losing Michael was one of the many life-altering moments that created the unique tapestry of who I am. Working with children, adults, and their families in end-of-life care for as many years as I have, you begin to realize just how short and fragile life is. Life forms from a series of decisions made from past experiences until you invite new ones. Tragedies, hardships, and unplanned detours happen to the best of us. We may not completely control our environment's happenings, but we can choose how we respond. I am not different.

I come to you today as a vulnerable and grieving mother. There are days I convince myself he is away at college. Other times I find myself almost questioning if Michael was real. Most of the time, thoughts of love and gratitude fill my soul. Memories play in my head like the flickering light of an old-fashioned film projector displaying pictures of a life once lived. Every moment spent in a world without your person can seem impossible-devastation, heartbreak, anger, denial, resentment, and hopelessness. The list is long, and the pain is deep. Despite all that, the cost of loving someone is always worth the price. Grief is a normal response to loss where love lives. I promise you hope, peace, and happiness are flourishing in the hearts of the grieved and for you too. This is my journey of loss, love, and transforming pain into purpose. Gratitude and grief can occupy the same space as love and loss do too.

Forgiving the unforgivable may seem nearly impossible. Frankly, a 'get outta jail free card' for those who have wronged us ends up releasing you from the chains of anger and resentment. Michael lives in a place of light and love. If I want to continue to sense Michael's love and presence, I need to create an equally bright world abundant with love. Anger and resentment would hinder me from feeling him and relating to me as I currently do. That is a price I am not willing to pay.

Continuing to live with purpose proves to me how imperative it is to reflect on the past, live in the present, and allow the future to echo applied wisdom. Many of us have experienced trauma throughout our lives. Some of us are more vulnerable to grief and trauma than others, and that's okay. Certain trauma can create reactions both now and later. That is when PTSD can take over a person's life, making it nearly inconceivable for life to have any joy and fulfillment. When I hear the neighbor pull up on their motorcycle and park, my subconscious mind still thinks, just for a moment, that Michael is home. Anytime I am commuting and a motorcyclist races past my car, I get anxious and hyper-aware of my surroundings. It's all a part of my new journey.

Eventually, I hope more of Michael's recipients find it in their hearts to respond to my letter. Naturally, I am incredibly grateful for Harold and our family's relationship. We bond through Michael's gift of life; nothing will ever change that.

My other children continue to live happy, joyful lives in spite of their grief. Each of them is growing from wounded siblings into grateful adults, celebrating their comradery as siblings. Now and then, one of them will say, 'Mom, do you think Michael is proud of me?" You know the answer.

Pictures of Michael continue to bring me joy, knowing I had eighteen amazing years with this kid. My photos, childhood videos, and Pizza Hut scented T-Shirts remind me how grateful I am that I had the time I had to be Michael's momma.

I chose not to live in the coulda, woulda, shoulda world. It isn't healthy, and it isn't productive.

My hope for you, my dear reader, is that you will find hope and inspiration within these words and open yourself to the possibility that grief can be one of your greatest gifts. When looking back on my life, I take the opportunity to recognize the times when I cultivated the most personal growth. The times I endured the most painful, terrifying, and life-altering experiences. Each one of those experiences allowed me to develop my personal power. Each time I said I couldn't, it was too hard, and it hurt too much; somehow, I did. I created a 'tool' I would need to get me through the next lesson.

There is so much more to my story. We will save that for another time. Until then, remember you are never alone in your grief. Do things that feel good for you. Talk to people, share your feelings and permit yourself to grieve. You are who you are in spite of and despite all the pain and suffering in your life. It made you who you are today; scars are proof of a battle won.

Courtney Kaplan

As the only child, Courtney was the center focus of her loving parents. By the age of four, Courtney found herself having to adjust to their divorce. Courtney found herself torn between two worlds. One parent became involved with the Jehovah's Witnesses while the other parent strongly disagreed with the teachings and influences. Courtney spent her impressionable years confused and vulnerable to the rhetoric and lifestyle requirements within the restrictive sect. At the age of nineteen, Courtney had a child out of wedlock, resulting in a forced separation from the JW's called being disfellowshipped. Religious family and friends could no longer associate with Courtney, disowning and rejecting her as a punishment for the birth of her child.

Courtney began her professional path as a nursing assistant. This laid the foundation for her passion to care for others. Courtney soon married, having four children in five years. Quickly, her family grew, bringing its own challenges. After six years of marriage, Courtney divorced with primary legal custody of her children. At the age of two, Courtney's youngest child displayed behaviors and abilities similar to those of Autism. Advocating and supporting her daughter's needs became center focus and still is to this day. Courtney continued to pour her time and resources into her career and her family. Courtney completed courses towards a degree as a registered nurse. She put schooling on hold to focus on family needs. With a successful career in medical sales, life experience trumped higher learning.

She lost her eighteen-year-old son in a tragic motorcycle accident. His injuries gave way to organ, tissue and eye donation. Her son made the unselfish choice to be an organ donor at the age of seventeen. Ultimately saving the lives of eight people and enhancing the lives of countless others. Courtney found herself with an opportunity to share her hope and strength with others becoming a volunteer at Nevada Donor Network, her local organ procurement agency. It is here, Courtney discovered that grief and gratitude can exist in the same space. Courtney shares her personal journey of loss and the gifts of grief through speaking on stages, as a best-selling author, and with group support organizations; leading Courtney to discover her true purpose and passion.

courtneybkaplan@gmail.com
702-628-0510

Made in the USA
Monee, IL
05 February 2023

26465757R00138

The Lemonade Stand 3

Publisher
Lemonade Legend Publishing

Michelle Faust
Lemonade Legend
www.lemonadelegend.com/the-lemonade-stand
Lemonade Legend Publishing

This book is dedicated to storytellers all over the world. There is beauty and wisdom in your experiences. I applaud those of you who have the courage to come forth.

I also dedicate the trilogy of The Lemonade Stand to God, Family, and Colleagues; for the guidance, encouragement, and patience I have received.

"Story, as it turns out, was crucial to our evolution -- more so than opposable thumbs. Opposable thumbs let us hang on; story told us what to hang on to." - Lisa Cron, Wired for Story